The Rugged Road

Theresa Wallach

With introduction and biographies by
Barry M Jones

D1557000

Panther Publishing

First Published by Panther Publishing Ltd in 2001
Panther Publishing Ltd, 10 Lime Avenue, High Wycombe, Bucks HP11 1DP, UK

Acknowledgements
I am indebted to many for their help in piecing together this brief biography of
two remarkable women and most especially to the following: Arizona State
University Foundation, The Brooklands Museum Trust, Wesley Warren Brown,
Peter Carter, *Chicago Daily News*, *Cycle Guide*, Geoffrey Dovico, Jessie Ennis
(née, Hole), Kris Slawinski, Derek MacLean, *The Motor Cycle*, *Motorcycling*,
David Powell, The National Motor Museum, The Panther Owners Club, The
Royal Geographical Society, Tessa Howard of The Vintage Motor Cycle Club,
Sheila Whittingham, The Women's Royal Army Corps Association, Womens
International Motorcycling Association, and of course the late Theresa Wallach,
herself.

Photographs and illustrations
Many of the photographs reproduced in this book have been extracted from
Theresa Wallach's original 16mm film of her journey by permission of the
Arizona State University Foundation. The quality of these images is poor but
in the publisher's opinion, it is better to have some original photographs of the
journey than none at all! Other photographs have been obtained from a variety
of sources identified in the list of illustrations where known. Every effort has
been made to trace and obtain the permission of the copyright owners but the
passage of time has made this extremely difficult. Some of these were probably
the property of Theresa Wallach herself.

The maps are taken from the 1:5 million survey maps, Afrique Feuille
Nos. 1, 3,4 and 5 (Service Geographique de l'Armée, 136 Rue de Grenelle,
Paris V11 circa 1930-3) by courtesy of the Royal Geographical Society.

ISBN: 978-09547912-9-2

Contents

Route

London (11 Dec. 1934) - Folkestone -Boulogne - Paris - Marseilles
Algiers - Blida - Djelma - Laghouat - Ghardaia
Ghardaia -El Golea (1 Jan. 1935) - In Salah
In Salah (7 Jan. 1935) - Arak - In Ecker (11 Jan. 1935) - Tamanrhassat
Tamanrhassat - In Guezzam (20 Jan. 1935)
In Guezzam - In Ahangarit - Tagguidda-n'Tesseoum - In Gal (25 Jan. 1935) - Agadez
Agadez (4 Mar. 1935) Tassaoua (West of Zindar) - Katsina (11 Mar. 1935) - Danbatta -
Kano - Potiskum - Damagum - Murbe - Damaturu - Ngumbdu - Beni Sheik - Kesawa - Maid
    - Giari - Mufi - Kaba Belge (Chad Border) - Kousseri - Fort Lami - Bousso - For
    Archambault
Fort Archambault (19 Apr. 1935) - Bangassou - Bondo - Buta - Ekibondo (30 Apr. 193
    Ituri Forest - then unclear as to actual route until - Beni - Lubero - Mt Ruwenzo
    Masaka - Mitalamite - Kampala
Nairobi - Arusha (5 June 1935) - Mt Kilimanjaro - Dodoma - Iringa (11 June 1935) - M
    Lusaka - Victoria Falls (Livingstone) - Hwange - Bulawayo
Bulawayo - Beitbridge (11 July 1935) - Mesina - Pietersburg - Pretoria - Johannesburg (23
    1935) - Bloemfontain - Beaufort West - Paarl (28 July 1935) - Cape Town (29 July 1

Florence's Return Journey: not detailed

Cape Town (18 Sep. 1935) - Salisbury - Nairobi - Faradje (due North of Mt Ruwenz
Niangara - Bula (Nov 1935) - Fardje - Marouna (presumably Maroua South West of Maid
- Kano (end of journey January 1936).

Illustrations

Preface

Having researched my first book on Phelon & Moore Ltd., manufacturers of the famous Panther motorcycle, I was determined to discover more about the epic Trans-Saharan crossing by Theresa Wallach and Florence Blenkiron in 1935. Fortunately for me, the late Bob Currie of *The Motor Cycle* had recently been in contact with Theresa and gave me her address. There then followed a 15 year 'pen-pal' friendship between Theresa and myself, during which time I encouraged her to have her account of this adventure published. She had in fact already started on the mammoth task of recording memories, extracting information from her detailed log book and reviewing still and cine films - some of which had still not been developed! Her manuscript *The Rugged Road* was then in its early stages.

It took her many frustrating attempts and rewrites to find a publisher sufficiently interested in publishing her work. In late 1998 she wrote to me saying that, fingers crossed, she had hopefully found a publisher on whom she could rely and that she would let me know as soon as everything was crystal clear. All went quiet, which was not unusual, but when I sent her a copy of my latest book, *The Panther Story*, I received a letter from her executor telling me that Theresa had died on her 90th birthday, 30th April 1999.

As a mark of respect to her, I then set about trying to locate her manuscript in the hope of getting it published in her memory. In due course and with help from her executors, the Arizona State University Foundation(to whom her effects had been bequeathed), Rollo Turner of Panther Publishing Ltd., and with some additional help from WIMA, my ambitious dream came true.

Unfortunately when the manuscript arrived, it saddened me to realise that contrary to earlier expectations, she had recorded so very little of her extraordinary life both before and after the adventure. Her two and a half year trek across America after the war was missing. I have since tried to complete these missing links by piecing together recollections in her letters to me and would be grateful for any further information particularly photographs, in order that this unique record on Theresa and Florence may be completed.

The Publisher and I have, wherever possible, left Theresa's account of the *Rugged Road* journey in her own words and style of writing.

BMJ
June 2001

Panther M100 similar to that used by Theresa Wallach and Florence Blenkiron

Introduction

by Barry M Jones

Theresa Elizabeth Wallach was born on April 30th, 1909. Her father, Henry Wallach is believed to have been of German extraction. He was a Fellow of the Royal Geographical Society and contributed many articles to the society's journal. His greatest contribution was in the closing years of the 19th century when he mapped for the first time, the West African territories.

The family home, 'The Woodlands', was in Dadford, north east of Buckingham, close to Stowe Park, which was the residence of the Dukes of Buckingham. It was a large house, surrounded by trees and undulating woodland. Over the years, her father had accumulated a large collection of souvenirs from his travels in the unheard of parts of the Dark Continent of Africa and elsewhere. He had truly travelled far. As a young man he went to the Canary Islands and explored the Gayadeque mountains where he excavated a 15th century skull of the ancient Guancho tribe of Tenerife.

The main collection was housed in a large room which had been extended by the demolition of a party wall. It was full of inscribed silver foils from Turkey, ceremonial shields and assegai spears from the Fulani and Zulu tribes of Africa. There were also ceremonial swords from India and daggers from the Somalian Dervish tribes. Parchments bearing text from the Koran were framed in ebony and mother of pearl while inlaid tables and Bukhara prayer mats gave the room a truly oriental feel.

Turkish divans, Arabian donkey saddles and Moroccan hand engraved and embossed brass trays stood on wooden trestles on a Persian carpet. There were many Egyptian artifacts; a mummified Egyptian cat from the 7th dynasty and a mummified Hawk - their sacred God, Bast. There was filigree from Assyria, Phoenician glass, African drums, clothing from China, Russia and Japan. The inventory was endless.

He had also explored the native Indian territories of Southwest America and returned home with pieces of Pueblo Indian pottery, discarded horse's mouth bits from the desert, a banderilla dart from the Toreador at a bull fight in Mexico, a cactus pod. He even had some Mitztake pottery presented to him by Governor Pimental of Oaxaco, Mexico.

Henry's collection was regarded as one of the finest private displays of archaeological and anthropological interest in the country. Theresa was awe stuck by the vastness of his collection and of his tales of adventures, but being two years

1

younger than her brother Charlie, she could not grasp as much of what she heard or fully appreciate the detailed placards accompanying the exhibits. Doubtless many a tale will never be retold.

Theresa's sense of adventure was thus instilled into her at a very early age and many a wet day was spent in her father's museum enacting fantastic journeys to Africa, Asia and the Americas. The house also held a large library which proved to be the warmest room in the house and cold days were often spent here admiring her fathers' sporting trophies – antlers, lion skins and elk horns, or reading those books on the lower shelves which she was able to reach! She became mesmerised by the early hand drawn maps, pictures of Zulu warriors, Pygmies, nomads and views of the Grand Canyon with American cowboys, of American Indians and their hogans, in which they lived.

An early interest in engineering grew from watching her father refilling accumulators, making bells ring and lights glow. Indeed as a young girl she soon found herself pretending that her first doll's pram was a motor car! In the summer months she helped out at the harvest giving a hand to the grooms and farm labourers as they reaped the hay with scythes and hoisted the sheafs by pitchfork onto the waiting wagons. Her brother was by now enrolled in the Boy Scouts and many a summer evening would be spent camping in the field, cooking by field kitchen and using semaphore to announce that the meal was ready!

Her father's appreciation of the West African geology lead him to take an interest in mining, for he believed that large reserves of gold would be found there. But no detailed maps yet existed of the Gold Coast, Ivory Coast, Ashanti reefs or Togoland, so he set about exploring the area. Henry Wallachs' maps were first published in 1901 and as a result, many private mining companies soon found a ready supply of investors through the London Stock Exchange, of which Henry was a member. The first successful deep shaft mines were sunk in Wassau and Ashanti at the turn of the twentieth century.

With his new found wealth, Henry and the family moved soon after the Great War to a farm in Wembley, North London. It was here that Theresa received her formal schooling at the Kilburn and Brondesbury High School for Girls. She also learnt to play the piano and piano organ at her aunts and at the age of 14 years had passed the Higher Division of the Royal College of Music's exams. Her cousin was Paul Rubens, a contemporary composer of musical plays and light operas. His works, *Miss Hook of Holland* and *King of Cadonia* met with rapturous applause at both The Prince of Wales and Adelphi theatres in London.

Fate

But some of those pictures of Africa she saw in her father's library showed young girls who remained untaught; their status to walk behind their menfolk and perform menial tasks for the tribe's daily routine. This may have aroused Theresa's feelings of injustice at the social standing of women and it began to nag at her conscience. She soon found the established and to her, old fashioned Victorian customs and tutelage, oppressive and at an early age vowed to follow her own destiny and way in life - relying on fate alone to guide her.

While living in Wembley during the great depression of the late 1920s, she used to watch people rushing out of their offices or factories to stand in line at the bus stop ready for their home journey. Used to the joy and freedom of the countryside, such a mundane urban life and limited offerings for women disheartened her so much that she decided that she would most certainly never lead such a life herself!

She talked to her parents about her dreams of adventure, of exploring Africa, the Grand Canyon, Paris, just as her father had done. But they were, to say the least, 'displeased' with her ideas, for they had assumed she would settle down to be a dutiful home-maker, as society demanded. She in turn felt that they were behind the times in saying it was wrong for a girl to have such silly notions - but, as Theresa also discovered, it was to be the same at her girls' school, where her friends told her she should have more sense than to talk about travelling to other countries, let alone continents!

Fortunately, she hadn't! So she set about doing something to fulfil her dreams. Determined to be free from the accepted formalities of the day, she sneaked her brother's bicycle out of the shed and taught herself to ride. While most girls were looking for suitors, Theresa found herself staring wide eyed at motorcycles rather than admiring the young leather clad men who rode them! Her parents were dismayed and tried once again to get Theresa to conform.

Such chastisements lead to many an argument. Much to her surprise though, in 1928 her domineering father agreed to her embarking on an Engineering course at the University of London. This esteemed University incorporated University College, London which, in 1878, was the first to accept women undergraduates. While most undergraduates would come together for socialising at tea and lunch breaks or walk together through the University buildings to get from classroom to classroom, Theresa would disappear down to the boiler house and thence around the back of the building and pass the rows of student's motorcycles. She soon found friends among her male motorcycling classmates, especially when asked by one of the assembled riders, which was her machine? Embarrassed, she stammered that she didn't have one, at which this friendly motorcyclist immediately offered to teach her to ride. Stephen Turner's offer was the start of her incredible motorcycling career.

Her first lesson was held along a deserted lane, but like most novice riders, she found it easy to go straight ahead yet impossible to turn around! She also soon learnt that there was no fun in riding a motorcycle in a skirt and she chuckled to herself as she recited one of her cousin Paul's lyrics, sung to her by her Nanny when much younger:

I've a little pink petty from Peter
And a little blue petty from John.
I've one green and yellow from some other fellow
And one that I haven't got on.

I've one made from pretty red flannel
That came from an Amsterdam store.
But with all the string and buttons and things,
Oh Dear! - I can't dance (ride) anymore.

Never again would she ride with one hand on the hand gear lever while holding down her flapping shirt. She got used to being reproved by her parents for wearing unladylike trousers, but never let on the reason why. It was soon after that with Stephen's help, she bought a second hand BSA Blue Star motorcycle. However as she was still living at home on the family farm with her parents, she made sure she parked the machine well out of sight in an old shed, walking into the house 'on time' as if she was still commuting by train! After a couple of weeks and by now tired of sneaking the motorcycle home, she parked it in the garden and 'disappeared' for a walk. On her return, she found her parents discussing the machine, believing it to be her brother Charlie's and agreeing that he most certainly was not going to keep it! When Theresa owned up, her distraught parents tried once more to persuade her to settle down and give up her unladylike attitude, for if she didn't, they said, she would be nobody's bride. Unfortunately this only lead to another massive argument and in tears, Theresa finally left home.

Jumping ahead a few years, Theresa visited Germany on holiday to meet her paternal relatives with whom she still maintained contact. This was probably in 1934. It was here that she met the Prince of Wales (later King Edward VIII) and was proudly presented with a signed photograph. At the time, the President of the German Republic was Paul von Hindenburg, but in 1933 a young Adolph Hitler, as leader of the National Socialist party made an abortive attempt to gain power; however Hindenburg offered him the post of Chancellor. On Hindenburg's death in August 1934, Hitler immediately declared himself *Führer* of Germany and overnight the streets were transformed from a staid Germanic style to a flourish of red and black Nazi flags. Theresa work up the next morning to this spectacle and horrified, she made her excuses and returned to England; it was for her one of the saddest days of her life.

Graduation

On graduating in 1932, Theresa progressed to drawing office design and practical machine shop experience with British Thompson Houston (BTH) at Willesden. But she remained restless. This was the age of the feminist movement and a group of graduates had formed the Womens' Engineering Society. At an Air Show in Southampton, lady pilots flying light aircraft gave a demonstration and for the target, Theresa volunteered to ride her motorcycle at a steady speed along the runway, to be dive-bombed by bags of powdered chalk. Who ever was closest, won - but luckily for Theresa, there were no direct hits!

Theresa later joined the London Ladies Motorcycle Club . This club was established by Jessie Hole in 1926 and was a select group of about seven lady riders who revelled in their motorcycling. It was they who arranged for the first ladies race at Brooklands in 1928. Theresa very soon discovered that she still had an awful lot to learn about riding motorcycles, especially when she entered with the Club in the London-Brighton run and soon found herself left far behind her fellow lady riders! Though the ladies got on well together and felt they were much of a par, it appears that Theresa was much more determined to succeed than to sit back and enjoy the fun of the club events. She also joined the International Motorcyclists Touring Club, embarking on all manner of motorcycle sports and events. She enjoyed many trials, scrambles and race-track events at the Brooklands track, where she soon found herself alongside many other women riders in the winner's circle. Her first race was in 1932, an event for which she inadvertently volunteered on mishearing an announcement at a club meet! It turned out to be for a Women's road race at Brooklands, but rather than face the embarrassment of admitting her mistake, she signed up. She tuned her BSA motorcycle herself and raised the compression ratio for extra power. Much to her surprise she won and was awarded a trophy donated by Sir Malcolm Campbell, himself a land speed record breaker.

Florence Blenkiron

Florence Blenkiron was born in Richmond, Yorkshire on 24th April 1904. She also held an early passion for motorcycles and took her first ride at the age of 16 years. Jessie Hole, who later became a works rider for New Imperial, and now in her 90s, recalled her first meeting with Florence at the first ladyies race at Brooklands in 1928. This race was organised by Lady Malcolm Campbell with her husband's blessing and full support. Riding her 350cc Raleigh, Jessie was the last off from the starting grid, but she soon realised someone else was there who shouldn't have been as another rider shot by; it was Florence Blenkiron mounted on Bill Lacey's Grindlay-Peerless. Jessie ended up almost half a mile behind her! It is believed Florence was at that time engaged to Bill. It is possible Florence joined the London Ladies Motorcycle Club at around this time.

Florence, a petite and truly remarkable young lady soon became a very competent rider and mechanic, though she kept herself to herself. In later years, she partook of many motor-car trials and events. By contrast Theresa showed no interest in four wheels despite having learned to drive a small pick-up, on the empty streets at the crack of dawn, when helping Craddock's Farm deliver milk churns to the market in Wembley. Theresa found gear changing on a motorcycle helped considerably when driving a car!

The next time Florence appeared at Brooklands was in 1933 and it appears she first met Theresa in what was then very much a male preserve, a Three-leg Junior All-Comer's Handicap race on 30th September 1933. Theresa was the only other woman club member present, entered as No.16, while Florence was No.17. This chance encounter was to prove memorable in more ways than one; Theresa missed the lining up bell and Florence, on her 346cc AJS, ran out of fuel on the last lap! But Florence made up for her mishap on 18th October, 1933 at Brooklands when she won a Three-lap All-Comer's Handicap race at 76.62mph on her AJS. That same day, no less than six BMCRC Gold Awards were awarded to male riders for breaking the magical 100mph barrier.

Their mutual enthusiasm for motorcycling drew the two lady riders closer together and soon they were joining other motorcycle clubs gaining a wonderful experience in trials riding, track events, touring. They even learnt trick riding by learning from and watching expert riders at trade sponsored national trials and events. In later years, when Theresa ran her motorcycle shop in Chicago, it was not unknown for her to perform the 'Arabesque' on her BSA motorcycle!

The 1930s were very much the 'Golden Years' of motoring, motorcycling and aviation. Women in particular were inspired to take part, especially following the example of Amy Johnson, who took up flying in 1928 and made her solo flight to Australia in 1930 followed by a flight to South Africa in 1932. The Auto Cycle Union, the governing body of motorcycling, organised sporting events for professional and amateur club members. This gave the motorcycle manufacturers of the time the opportunity to compete against each other in arduous sporting events and six day trials in which many lady riders took part. Florence and Theresa competed in several 24 hour trials as well the London-Gloucester MCC nighttime trials through the Cotswolds and Forest of Dean, all of which demanded considerable skill and judgment. As their expertise grew, they began winning more trophies.

'Moto-ball' was a popular spectator sport of the time. While it was hard on both the rider and machine, it brought in much needed revenue and publicity for the many amateur motorcycle clubs. It was claimed to be the fastest game of football in the world and much reliance was placed on the rider's ability to maintain perfect balance and control over the motorcycle, while he (or she!) kicked the ball. Avoiding collision could only by achieved by moving the rider's body and weight about the machine, like a contortionist and indeed these vital skills were to play a fundamental part in the success of Theresa's later Motorcycle Riding School teaching methods.

On April 14th 1934, Florence became the first woman to break the magical 100mph barrier on a motorcycle. This was achieved at 102.06mph on the second lap of a Three-lap All-Powers Outer Circuit Handicap race at *The Motor Cycle* Clubman's day meeting at Brooklands, riding a 500cc Grindlay Peerless. This was fitted with an Eric Fernihough prepared 500cc JAP dirt track engine. It is interesting to note that the Brooklands entry sheet shows Florence was due to ride her 346c AJS! The Club wisely permitted only two lady riders on this heat, Florence and a Miss Mooret who rode a 500cc Ariel. Though Florence broke the 100mph barrier, Mooret actually won the heat at 90.88mph as Florence pulled out immediately after lap two, having secured her Gold! Theresa was also present that day and had hoped to attempt the 100 mph record herself on C.T. Atkin's Douglas motorcycle, but at the last minute he withdrew the Douglas, saving it for a later race. Theresa was not amused.

For her achievement, Florence was awarded the British Motor Cycle Racing Club's Gold Star Award. In recording the event, *Motorcycling* described her as 'Wonder Girl' - and went on to describe the day's events by saying, "Spectacular though the feats of several clubmen were, they paled somewhat by the sensational 102mph lap by a lady Beemsee member, Miss F M Blenkiron .... the first of her sex to claim the BMCRC's Gold Star badge."

Only two other women gained that award, Beatrice Shilling on an ohc Norton, some months after Florence's record and Theresa Wallach in 1939, who rode at 101.64 mph on a borrowed Francis Beart prepared 348cc Norton. Though several other women riders gained considerable fame on the race track, it would be many more years before they too would achieve the same celebrity status as their male counterparts. Lady riders did particularly well in trials and the Six Day events, sponsored by the motorcycle manufacturers. One such was Marjorie Cottle who rode for Raleighs alongside Jessie Hole's brother. Jessie also enjoyed trick and stunt riding and, being intrigued by an American stunt rider who used to ride through plates of glass, decided to do this same trick in England, with the help of her brother. The first time was with one pane of glass and on another with two! They hoped that the panes of glass would survive the journey to the venue! Needless to say, few others were keen enough to try the trick for themselves! It is fair to say that most lady riders excelled because they enjoyed riding and taking part, though Theresa was much more forthright about her ambition to win and the press certainly did give fair coverage to those lady riders who deserved credit.

Planning the Adventure

'Blenk', as Florence was affectionately known, was then living in Sanderstead, near Croydon in Surrey, and had for some time been trying to get to South Africa to catch up with family members, but when her closest friend Faye also decided to emigrate, she became rather distraught. When asked what the problem was, Theresa suggested Florence should go by motorcycle, to which Florence snappily replied, "Don't be funny!", but soon followed this up by asking, "Would you come with me?". As time ticked by, Theresa once again asked, "Well, Blenk, what about it?". "What about What?" came the reply, to which Theresa explained, "... when do we start - we have nothing to lose except our heads to head hunters!"

The seeds for their epic journey were sown.

Blenk was secretary to the Technical Assistant to the Chairman of the large Sheffield based iron and steel company, Hadfields Ltd. As the office manager, she had become a good organiser - she even organised a year's leave for the venture! Theresa was confident that with her own engineering background, she could take care of the motorcycle in almost any circumstance.

To Theresa, a motorcycle was the very embodiment of travel and adventure - after all, that was what life was all about. She would make the most of her time filling her days with riches of a different kind, more precious than any material assets and record in her memory and by log book, stories of her adventure - her childhood dreams were about to turn into reality.

They spent just over a year planning and making preparations while seeking as much information as possible about Africa. The Sahara is the largest desert in the world covering some three and half million square miles. Their route was to start in Algeria, which at that time was a French colony and all routes crossing the Sahara desert came under the jurisdiction and surveillance of the French Government and military, from whom permission had to be obtained to cross each region.

Since time immemorial, camel caravans and camel trains had crossed the great Sahara guided by veiled traders and nomadic tribesmen, free to roam as they pleased, heading from oasis to oasis, known only to them.

The Sahara was still considered barely passable by anything other than camels, but in the early 1920s, a French expedition, using specially prepared caterpillar tracked cars, prospected a direct route due south from Algiers, through the Hoggar mountains and thence to Kano, in British Colonial Nigeria. Wells were sunk along the way, ranging in distance between 250 miles and 500 miles apart. These wells are still marked on the Michelin road maps of Africa. The quality of water varied at these wells and the depth at which potable water can be found is marked on these maps. The longest span was south of The Tropic of Cancer, between the Tamanrhassett and Agadez oases.

In 1933 an unprepared motorcar was driven along this route and its success demonstrated this to be the most feasible way of gaining access to the interior of the great continent of Africa. Despite many warnings, Blenk and Theresa were still seriously prepared to test their own endurance and go by motorcycle across the Sahara and thence to Cape Town. Indeed their determination grew stronger the more they realised they would be the first to complete a north-south crossing of the Sahara and African continent by motorcycle. They aimed to follow all that remained of the recent car tracks. It may well have been a reckless idea, but at least it would be an adventurous one!

Not surprisingly, neither the motorcycle trade nor anyone else could be persuaded to give them assistance or sponsorship, especially as these were two women which made it all the more frustrating! They had at least consoled themselves with the thought that since no one was likely to sponsor them, they would have to do it themselves and treat this like any other of their many trails events! Almost everyone frowned at the very idea of their adventure - "You are going WHERE?" - "You'll never get there". Even the more technically minded ventured that an air cooled engine could not survive the desert heat - it had never been done before and they would not even attempt it themselves!

Of course at the time, neither Theresa nor Blenk fully understood or appreciated the dangers and hardships that these well meaning people were trying to explain. Theresa freely admitted many years later, that even if they had known, they would probably still have gone anyway!

Finding a suitable motorcycle posed a few problems. They could have bought one themselves, but appreciated that considerable work might be necessary to make it suitable for the crossing, so they would be better off securing sponsorship from one of the motorcycle manufacturers. Unfortunately for them, a couple of years earlier a private rider had secured help from Vincents for a round the world tour, but had suffered endless breakdowns and difficulties. Vincents eventually decided to withdraw their help at which the stranded rider vowed to 'make their name mud around the world'. As a result, the British Motor Cycle and Cycle Manufacturer and Trades Union revised their policy to prevent any further blackmail. Their new policy was emphatic; its members would not undercut other traders by selling below the manufacturer's recommended retail price nor would they entertain unfair competition by offering other incentives. In other words, they should not respond to the many requests for patronage from Clubs or enthusiastic individuals in their escapades. Nearly every motorcycle manufacturer and dealer was a member of this powerful Union, and indeed without this membership they were unable to take a stand at the crucial annual Olympia motorcycle show.

But one pioneering manufacturer, and indeed a founder member of the Union, had already run into problems with the Union. That company was Phelon & Moore Ltd of Cleckheaton, Yorkshire, whose membership had already been suspended. Phelon & Moore had fallen foul of the Union by negotiating a special deal with Pride & Clarke, a London motorcycle dealer, who were already in the Union's bad books for selling below manufacturers recommended prices! The deal would allow Pride & Clarke to sell P&M's new 250cc and 350cc lightweight Panther models at a huge discount. This came about during the recession of the early 1930s which severely hit P&M's fortunes. In 1932 Frank Leach had designed a small 250cc motorcycle to replace P&M's earlier, but extremely expensive Panthette V-twin. His new 250cc model would hopefully transform P&M's fortunes, but initial sales were poor and it was not until Pride & Clarke, recognising the potential of this new model, offered to negotiate sole distribution rights that P&M secured a guaranteed outlet with no marketing or advertising costs, but it came at price. Though profits would be low, cash flow was secure, but their Union membership would be lost and dealings with suppliers might be put in jeopardy. As events were to prove, Pride & Clarke's new 'Red Panther' sold like hot cakes - at £29/17/6d it was the cheapest, fully equipped 250cc motorcycle on the market. P&Ms future was secure.

As Phelon & Moore were no longer bound by the Union's rules, they showed considerable interest in the two ladies. Even though as a company they had considerable experience in trials work and exporting to many commonwealth countries, which had similar environments, it took some persuading before P&M's Richard Moore and Bertram Marians succumbed to these resolute women. However they were not prepared to go out of their way in making something special and offered the ladies a copy of their catalogue from which to chose a suitable model. In fact P&M were already developing an improved version of their famous 600cc single cylinder Panther, which was to have had several new features on both engine and frame. One such was a new enlarged sump with external cooling fins - the trans African crossing could prove to be a bonus to them in proving and developing the model further.

P&M's side-valve 3-1/2hp motorcycle combination had been adopted as the standard mount by the Royal Flying Corps in the Great War and they were renowned for their reliability and durability. Their later overhead valve 'Panther' motorcycles were also pioneering machines with a well respected touring and sidecar performance. The P&M was unique - the engine formed a structural part of the frame, there being no conventional front down tube. This arrangement produced an immensely strong design. Furthermore the P&M engines used a dry sump construction in which lubricating oil was pumped from a forward mounted sump and was returned by being flung forward into the sump by the rotating flywheels; this helped both engine cooling and reduced flywheel drag. The 600cc Panther was an ideal mount. Blenk had already ridden Panthers in many trials events and already owned a black and orange painted Panther/Watsonian combination, which in July 1934, won the William Watson Cup for smartest combination at the Watsonian Rally, Birmingham.

Gaining support from other sponsors was fraught with problems as most of the potential sponsors were governed by the manufacturer's Union and news of P&M's involvement could have made matters worse for them if they were to associate with a debarred Union member! Those who were brave enough to accept were also wary of being associated with potential failure and adverse publicity. Indeed even Lord Wakefield (of Castrol oils), at that time a very prominent sponsor, preferred not to be associated for that very reason, though he had agreed as early as 1928 to sponsor Jessie Hole in her own ambition to cross the Sahara and conquer Africa.

In due course other sponsors came to their assistance with Watsonian supplying the sidecar and trailer, John Edgington, the tent, while various clothing manufacturers supplied tropical outfits and special lead-foil lined and quilted topee helmets. On the technical front, Prices supplied their Motorine B oil and grease, Lodge supplied spark plugs. All hoped to gain valuable publicity along with those others who supplied the standard components fitted to the Panther, such as Smiths, H. Terry etc.

The Venture

The sidecar was essentially a standard Watsonian touring model with long heavy duty flat leaf springs at the rear and coil springs at the front. The ladies had already accepted that a heavily laden trailer would only serve to hamper their efforts to cross the desert sands but with so little information to hand, they decided to play safe by carrying an extra week's supply of rations. A specially made steel cross-member was fitted to the rear of the sidecar chassis to accommodate a quickly detachable Rice spring loaded coupling with overrun brake for the flat topped, 6ft x 3ft8in x 12in deep, Watsonian tradesman's trailer. The leaf springs were specially long affairs. Accommodation was simply in the form of a specially adapted John Edgington tent erected on the trailer's flat top. It came complete with mosquito netting which draped down to ground level. The trailer top provided a very firm and secure bed.

By late November 1934, the entire outfit had been meticulously prepared at George Clarke Motors in Acton, under the expert guidance of former P&M technical engineer Frank Leach, who had left P&M in June 1933 to manage Clarke's Acton branch. The Panther Redwing Model 100 was essentially standard, though fitted with extra heavy duty Webb forks, stronger wheel spokes, wider mudguards to accommodate Fort Dunlop 3.50in car tyres and a Moseley block pillion saddle. Improved needle valve lubrication control to the valve gear and drive chains were also specified. The usual enclosed primary drive chain case was abandoned in favour of a simple top guard. The chain was to be lubricated in the manner of P&M's TT models by drip feed from a modified battery casing, mounted in its usual position, which served as an oil reservoir! The service battery was an Exide unit from an Austin 7 motor car and was located in the sidecar and was charged by a large car-type Miller dynamo. The gear ratios were specially adapted for low gear crawling with a 21.2:1 low and a 5.9:1 top ratio. One would have expected upswept trials pattern exhaust system but due to the intense heat of the Sahara desert, it was considered more prudent to keep the hot exhaust well away from the rider's legs!

On 30th November 1934, two weeks before their adventure began, Bertie Marians, P&Ms Sales Director, met Florence and Torrens of *The Motor Cycle*, at The Jolly Farmers Inn near Camberley, Surrey and presented her with the gleaming deep maroon red painted Panther 'Redwing' Model 100 combination, registered YG 7404. He gave them express instructions to "Please try and break it"! Frank Leach would be at hand later that day to carry out any necessary modifications - what confidence!

Indeed in the hands of Blenk and Torrens, they desperately tried to break it in a hair raising endurance exercise carried out in what can best be described as wreckless abandon, over the rugged Army training grounds near Bagshot Heath, Surrey, for which special permission had been granted. The first part of the destructive trial was along the rough heath land used in the Southern Scott Scrambles - they found it was perfectly possible to drive the combination and trailer at 40mph without having to cling on for dear life. Then they took to the heath and leaped and hopped over small ditches and through thorny scrub before coming to a wide gulch, with a drop of about six feet to the path, followed by a short scrubby track up a bank with a gradient of about 1:4. Then it was back onto a plateau with a further short, steep bank. For a trials rider this was sheer bliss, but what about the sidecar rider and trailer? The automatic over-run brakes on the trailer proved an asset in controlling the outfit, but an overcautious descent allowed the combination to come to ahalt at an awkward angle. However the diminutive Blenk found it quiet easy to manoeuvre the outfit back onto level ground. After one or two more 'tests' they returned contentedly to the Jolly Farmer Inn hoping to invite the others to come and join them, but they had other ideas and demanded they test the outfit on the notorious Red Road Hill. Torrens, knowing this notorious sandy hill, had visions of the combination getting half way up and then racing back down and collapsing into a mangled heap. Flat out in bottom gear, he raced the machine down one incline and up the other, only to get stuck about 20 yards up the hill, with the back wheel digging itself ever deeper into the sand until finally the Burgess silencers were themselves buried. A second attempt from a different angle on a slightly milder 1:4 ascent got them closer to the summit but come what may that summit remained unconquered. However they had achieved what they had set to out to prove; they had discovered no weaknesses. So, satisfied with the trials, they returned home bouncing across the heath like a gun tractor and carriage in rapid advance, only to become entangled in a gulch, which proved to be narrower than the trailer and they came to an abrupt halt, having struck a tree stump.

There was nothing for it but to unhitch the trailer and manoeuvre the outfit back onto firm ground. On the second attempt, they managed to drive out of the gulch in one piece. With this renewed confidence and as if possessed by demons, they then decided to return across the heath to the Inn at full pelt, bouncing in and out of pot holes and ditches with the trailer spending most of its time airborne! This mad caper proved too much for the poor engine, which had barely had time to run itself in properly and it suddenly died with a seized piston; but after a few minutes to cool, all was well and they continued in a more dignified manor.

The battered combination arrived at the inn and the waiting officials. As Torrens charmingly put it, "nothing serious *had* broken". Soon Frank Leach had the outfit back at Acton and repaired, ready for the epic adventure.

On December 11th, 1934, Theresa Wallach and Florence Blenkiron, complete with the heavily laden outfit, now christened *The Venture*, arrived at The Crown House, Aldwych, London, ready for their official send off by Lady Astor and the Acting High Commissioner of Southern Rhodesia.

The following chapters are Theresa's own account of their trans-African expedition from her manuscript, *The Rugged Road*.

The Rugged Road

Theresa Wallach

Algiers to Cape Town showing the route taken and major places on the way

The Start Of The Venture

Having finally obtained our passports, credentials and some French money, we were ready for Africa. On 11th December, 1934 Blenk and I left home in Ealing for The Crown House offices of the Southern Rhodesia Government, in London's Aldwych. This was to be our official departure point. Names of the places along our route to Cape Town were painted on the side of the deep maroon Panther combination, which had by now been christened, 'The Venture' - it certainly made people turn and glance and wonder at what they saw. At The Crown House, a number of dignitaries had gathered for their parting words of farewell. Lady Astor, an American who became Britain's first woman Member of Parliament, had herself been taught to ride a motorcycle from Lawrence of Arabia. She spoke to the audience saying that she wished she was coming too - if only to get away from the telephone! Lady Astor's message was quite foreseeing, "I am an unrepentant feminist and convinced that whatever a man can do, women can do too". However, she overlooked the fact that no one had yet undertaken our venture.

The Commissioner for British colonial Northern Rhodesia, Mr. B.F. Wright, said in a short speech, "These days we are accustomed to young women undertaking the seemingly impossible and emerging successful in the end". He went on to warn, "there is no doubt that you will encounter obstacles and difficulties... some of these have been pointed out, but you are still determined to carry on. You will pass through Southern Rhodesia in February, the rainy season, when two inches of rain sometimes fall within an hour and rivers swell threateningly to a height of fifteen to twenty feet above their normal level, flooding the countryside ... you will also meet lions and elephants".

Yes, we had heard of these hazards, but would have to pass through rains on some part of the journey. Other dignitaries and friends wished us 'Good Luck' and telegrams with good wishes from absent friends were thrust into our hands as were various small mementos, dropped into the already overladen sidecar. Among these little gifts was a silver horseshoe broach for each of us, a lucky four-leaf clover and a sprig of white heather. Other goodwill tokens tossed in at the last minute's excitement included a tape-measure to measure the distance to Cape Town and a Christmas pudding!

About a thousand Londoners saw us off, with a touch of real life drama far better than any film could convey. As we became overwhelmed by the fanfare farewell, a policeman with a gruff voice said, "Move along now please, we have made a way for you!" and several other London bobbies, determined to get us away, provided a motorcycle escort in front of and behind us, to thread our way

15

through the congested traffic. We were finally off to Africa! On the way to the channel port of Folkestone, the English weather favoured us as the sun tried to shine. That night we crossed the English Channel by ferry boat to the French port of Boulogne.

France

The rain had now turned to a steady drizzle. Over wet, straight, tree lined and mostly cobbled roads, on a cold winter's morning, the seventy-five miles to Paris was a dreary ride. The way to the Consulate Office in the French capital, riding on the right-hand side of the road, with the sidecar mounted on the 'wrong' side during rush-hour traffic, had some anxious moments.

We had yet to receive the official stamp of approval for permission to cross the Sahara desert in French colonial Algeria. The French embassy in London had declined to take responsibility in granting it and it seemed to us that the right place to get consent was in Paris. Instead, the authorities there said we should apply to the authorities at the Port de'Marseilles, before leaving the country. The bureau in Marseilles explained that the Algerian Office would still be the place to verify it, even if one had been given at Marseilles.

Half way through France, at Lyons, about two hundred and fifty miles south, while seated at a small table in a restaurant, on the far side of the dining room, our knee-boots and britches looked out of place amongst the fashionable Sunday dresses worn by the other lady patrons. Soon the Head Waiter came across the dining room to our table. "Gentlemen," he said graciously in perfect English, "... Gentlemen should wear jackets". Blenk, trying to translate the menu looked up and simply said in her feminine voice, "Is that so ?". We should have known that *grenouille* was the French for 'frogs', and when they arrived, I turned up my nose at my plate. Blenk remarked that when in France, be like the French - enjoy it!

Algiers

The steamship *Tingad* sailed from Marseilles to the Port of Algiers, our African starting place. Crossing the Mediterranean sea to a different land and life of adventure, was going to be a rough thirty-six hours voyage, but before we landed, I felt the warm, dry air and saw a cloudless blue sky. I soon left behind the memories of bleak English weather, unimportant affairs and the daily routine of the life, from not so long ago.

At the headquarters of the Société Algérienne des Transport Tropicaux, (SATT) at 20 Rue Sadi-Carnot, Algiers, the Director arranged for us to see the Captain of the northern region of Algeria for a permit to enter the Sahara and for him to approve our desert crossing. The Captain had never before been faced with an application like this, so we had to come back later with more information.

The St George Hotel, where reservations had been made for us, was a place of grandeur, with high walls and ornamental ceilings - just like a palace. In the mosaic tiled lobby, an Arab porter carried our kit bags and shoulder packs, stepping on cushiony oriental carpets and then up the wide stairway leading to our room. "A better room will be available for you tomorrow", he said in arab-anglaise, as he pushed open the solid-wood door. Flopping into a comfortable chair Blenk commented, "This is an expensive place!" After a rest, we walked outside, sight-seeing. I suggested saving the expense of dining-room meals and buying food to eat in our room. "We can't do anything like that!" she gasped. "Why not?", I tried to convince her, "who's to know?". We returned to the deluxe hotel like thieves in the night, with packets of food under our jackets. Having enjoyed a taste of local fare, we concealed the leftovers along the shelf inside the clothes closet and went out again for more sight-seeing.

Algiers was known as the 'City of White', as most buildings were white or light coloured. The air was so clean that they stayed that way and in the sunlight the whole town looked bright and cheerful. The sight of a turban-wearing policeman, in scarlet-lined cloak, mounted on an Arabian horse and veiled women among waifs, put us into the right frame of mind for our travels. We peered into a round domed building, which turned out to be a market place, where products from all parts of the East - carpets, elephant tusks, food, tea from India and all kinds of merchandise - were piled high to be sold by the merchants who had gathered there. We could see the stools where they sat and talked, making gestures, discussed and bargained, sounding like they were quarrelling, but it was their way of doing business and we pleasantly wasted some time waiting for a bargain to be settled.

I wish we had spent more time walking around the old-as-history kasbah's narrow streets, where one could reach out of the window of the weird little houses and touch hands with someone across the street, while a baggage-carrying donkey went along, below. The red fez headdress of Mohammedan countries looked familiar to me, as father had brought back a fez from Morocco and had worn it around the house. In a city street, a gentleman who evidently had been reading the newspaper, stopped us and inquired in good English, "Are you the two ladies intending to cross the desert on a motorcycle ?". He urged us, "change your mind and don't go - it is too dangerous". Friends, acquaintances and now strangers, echoed the same old story.

When we returned to the fabulous St George Hotel the desk clerk gave us the key to a better room, with a beautiful view overlooking the courtyard. In this new room, all the food we had been hiding was laid out along the closet shelf, exactly the same way as we had been hiding it; French bread, sausage, cheese, chocolate, fruit and mineral water, all in 'apple-pie' order. Nobody said a word. Silence means the same in any language!

The Captain of the French Foreign Legion regiment at the barracks, responsible for northern Sahara, wanted information about ourselves and specifications of the motorcycle and our equipment. He spoke English very well and understood as we explained our application for a permit to cross the Sahara. Although there was no doubt about our credentials, there were other things that concerned him, such as verification of physical fitness. He asked us how we intended finding the way to the next oasis water hole in the desolate expanse of sandy wasteland? How would we carry enough water in case of a breakdown? We answered his every question. He then examined the motorcycle. The air-cooled engine did not need water and if we got stuck in the sand, we could lift it out and push it. As for our physical condition, each of our medical affidavits certified we were fit and had received the required inoculations. Every disease that we had not got, was spelled out on the document in medical terms I am sure no lay-person could understand; he strained his eyes over it. The fee for the permit was four hundred francs. It included all six radio outposts, from one oasis to the next, that spanned the desert over a distance of about two thousand miles, stating that, "In the event of non arrival at the next oasis, within a specified time, a search would be ordered". The cost of a search party would be four francs per kilometre (each way), extra. To be rescued in the Sahara was apparently not a poor person's sport. The Registrar clerk did not speak English very well and neglected to enquire about our financial status!

Two weeks after leaving London, our application to cross the Hoggar region of the Sahara was finally ratified. Our departure from Algiers was delayed another day so that we could accept a kind invitation to a Christmas party at the home of a Port of Algiers official, Villa Aurelian in Parc Gatliff. Christmas Day in Algiers was celebrated around a Christmas tree where we met their family and friends - in Mohammedan Algeria, the coloured lights and pretty packages didn't seem so foreign. I remembered Christmas as a child was unusual too, for we had to entertain ourselves. A frosted tree was brought in from the woods to be decorated with carrots. Each horse was led from the stables to the patio, to walk around it and nip the carrots off. Here in Algiers, little gifts under the Christmas tree were for Blenk and me. Blenk accepted a pen and a pin-cushion donkey with a card "When you get stuck in the sand, get Jack to pull you out!". Extra strength boot laces for us, could be tied together in an emergency, to secure something on our journey. I still use the special tool given me, with blades inside the hollow handle. Then there were two small bottles of *haut goût* Cognac for us. The dining table was spread with roast gazelle, fresh vegetables, savoury dishes and everyone was cheerful. Then came the plumb pudding, the traditional English Christmas Pudding, with a flame of liqueur spirit to kindle the emotional spirit of goodwill and hospitality.

*The start of
The Venture*

Reaching The Desert
Algiers To Ghardaia Oasis

Boxing Day

At about ten o'clock in the morning on the day after Christmas, a large crowd gathered along the main street, Rue Michlet, to see us off. It would be the last time for us that clocks and split seconds would be of any concern. Every special task we had taken upon ourselves to do had been done satisfactorily and at long last we were ready to start the African expedition. We were escorted by French and Algerian representatives of the *Echo d'Algie* newspaper and local motorcyclists for the first thirty miles as the road climbed abruptly from the coast and passed through the village of Beni-Mared, as it cut through the Atlas Mountain range, where the highest peaks are snow covered all the year round. These mountains extend 1,500 miles between the coast and the Sahara desert, sealing off the African continent from the Mediterranean sea and Europe. Little streams of water splashed down over the rocks among the woody slopes and sometimes trickled across the road; anywhere else we would have seen rabbits scuttling around, but here we saw tailless monkeys in the trees. The slow-paced procession, with our small vehicle pulling a heavy load, wound upward through the curves on a black topped road until we reached the village of Blida, where it dissipated into a gravel track.

The cafe at the end of this road was our farewell place. We all sat down together for a snack around plain, but clean little tables. There was nothing much left to talk about. Again and again, even before leaving London, we had said "Good-bye" to someone or other, but it was never quite like this now - the last farewell.

A few perplexed Arabs looked on from a sandy quadrangle as we filled our four gallon fuel tank and one of the twenty-litre containers for the last time from a petrol pump. I forget who left first, but as our friends turned to return north, we continued south. Blenk was quiet. I don't know what she was thinking; probably the same as me, wondering about the reliability of our heavily laden motorcycle; or the extremes of weather, our health, diseases and all those things we had been warned about or of those mysterious black-eyed Bedouins who stared and stared - and stared. Would they be hospitable now that we were alone? We steered towards the unknown and sauntered along.

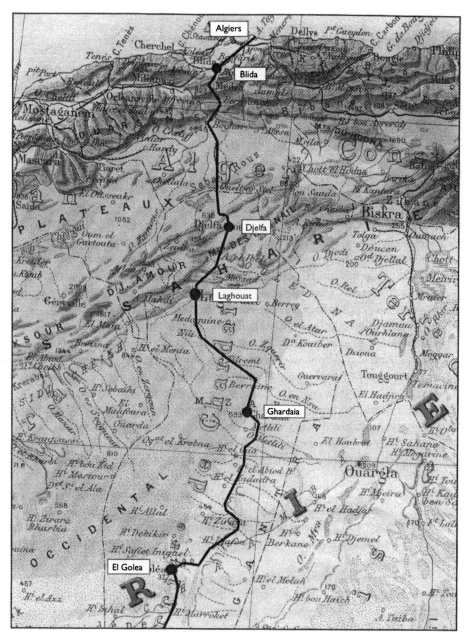

Algiers to El Golea showing the route taken by The Venture

The escort from Algiers

The Atlas Mountains

The track twisted and turned over rocky ground through the highest part of the pass to 4,000 ft, near Djelfa and by the end of the day, we descended onto loose stones and sand as the temperature dropped to a shivering cold.

Our first night of camping, before crossing the sparsely populated plain of the oasis of Laghouat, was a clumsy process as we bumped into each other as if there was not enough room out here! I soon discovered that the ridge poles to support the roof of the tent were nowhere to be found. Unfortunately they had been left behind somewhere, probably not being recognised as being part of our equipment, so we broke branches from a scanty tree and made a pair to serve our purpose. Making camp, repacking and preparing snacks each day took us far too long and required team work and much practice to reduce to the minimum the time lost if we were to make the most of the daylight to make good progress.

The next night, we found a good place to camp, near to where we could see a roof-top. Blank walked over there to ask for some water as we were not then carrying a full load, but now it was vital to carry more supplies in the trailer. A light was shining upstairs and there was someone in the house, but nobody answered. When Blenk knocked again, an elderly woman thrust her wary head out of the window and couldn't have been more startled even if Blank had got horns. To the sound of a lock and draw-bolt, the French woman opened the door and called, "Qu'est-ce que c'est?". I imagined Blenk stammering in her best French: "Water please - please can I have some water ?". She kindly filled the gallon container saying something like "Allez Algie, vite! It is not safe here at night where there are nomads" and promptly shut the door, not knowing we were in fact going the other way - to Cape Town. I lay thinking that night, before falling asleep, wondering what next we would encounter. Of a December morning, daybreak was quite late and it was still dark as we rode out of the hills, some two hundred and forty miles from Blida across the barren plain aiming to reach Laghouat oasis before sunset.

At noon we swapped places from saddle to sidecar - the change was as good as a rest. Along the way an Arab shepherd, wearing white *burnouse* and carrying his crook, turned to look back as he heard us coming and moved his flock to one side so we could pass by this most biblical of sights. Nomads learnt long ago that sheep thrive in the poorest pasture. Occasionally, gazelle on slender legs, leapt gracefully over the scrubs while bustards pecked the ground for food and would not move away until we were almost on top of them.

The deep sand and flint-rock track was as wide as it was long, as if heavy earth-moving equipment had haphazardly been at work all over the place. Someone who we met in Algiers and who seemed to know a lot about the desert, told us that big rocks had been set into place to form a straight line, indicating the direction to follow. Trailer-wag was a problem as we steered a winding path to avoid rocky outcrops but all we achieved was to slap a tyre against sharp flint-rocks causing us numerous punctures. Inner tubes were patched until beyond repair before a new one was fitted. These many delays prevented us from reaching Laghouat before nightfall. It was never advisable to ride into an oasis in darkness, so we pitched camp on the outskirts - so near and yet so far.

Laghouat

Apparently we had stopped that night near to the oasis, but close to a Bedouin tribal settlement. Although not a soul was in sight, dozens of eyes were still watching us. I was sheltering the Primus stove from a chill wind while boiling water for tea, when I saw sandaled feet walking towards us. Looking up, I could see their goat skin tents between the rocky outcrop and a cloaked nomad with rifle in hand, coming towards us. He touched the motorcycle and stretching out a probing hand over the shiny levers, touched the horn button. 'HOOT!,' went the horn. He jumped. I jumped. As luck would have it, the motorcycle held his attention while we went about our camping chores as usual.

Aroused by the goings-on, others from the settlement came over to us. They made no sound as their feet seemed to glide over the sand in the eerie light of dusk. We watched them, watching us. They looked beautiful - tall, veiled and dignified.

In these places, weapons were very much sought after and if these tribesmen knew we had firearms, it might have endangered us to the extent we would probably have been better off without them. Besides, in wilderness and jungle country, a revolver was not much protection against big game.

In truly becoming surroundings, I heard the wail of a flute coming from somewhere nearby and a humdrum male voice chanting the Koran. I knew the semblance of the Koran from a parchment we had in the small museum at home. I had to bend an ear to hear the Cantor warbling the *suras*, or verses, that reveal the Word of God, the Divine Scripture and faith of Moslems. Whether read or memorised, he had chosen that part for this evening's prayer.

At dawn they were back again, wearing the loose *Kaffiych* head cloth held in place by a braid of twisted camel hair placed around the head. Half hiding their cloaked faces, they gathered around us while we packed, checked everything, started the engine and slowly moved away. I turned around, not looking where I was going, to keep on eye on them long enough to see us safely out of their reach.

The first camel we saw in natural surroundings put a touch of drama to our morning's ride. They soon became a familiar sight and looked more lifelike than those we saw at the zoo. It seemed to be feeding on stones, but was actually finding sparse scrub growth almost concealed in the hollows. When a camel is really hungry it will eat almost anything, including rags. They can go without water for days, storing it in their humps to drink during dry spells and keep food in one of their stomachs. These extraordinary beasts of burden, with their shaggy brown hair, have served mankind for thousands of years.

In the ancient commune of Laghouat, on the northern fringe of the Sahara, we could see a white mosque on a hill, amidst palm trees against the blue sky. It was a busy little place and by mid-morning the market place was crowded and craftsmen at stalls seemed to be going about their work for the pleasure and satisfaction of doing it. Arab boys were selling three day-old *Echo d'Algie* newspapers which had reported our departure from Algiers. People now recognised us and as we rode past, soldiers of the French Foreign Legion stood to attention and shouldered-arms in salute. Those who could read looked over the names of places painted all over our sidecar, showing the way to Cape Town. We walked around the market place shopping for provisions, watched metal-workers and embellishers of leather saddles and admired their handicraft. There were potters shaping ceramics and colourful fabric stalls, but we had neither the money to spare for souvenirs nor spare space to carry non-essential items. We bought dates, bread, cans of fruit, beans and then filled our water containers and fuel cans ready for the next one hundred and thirty mile leg of our journey, to Ghardaia oasis in the M'Zab, our first official Sahara wireless outpost.

The direction to Ghardaia, on the northern edge of the Sahara, was marked by a pile of rocks each about four feet high, placed at regular intervals of a kilometre apart. To go any further and not see another marker, meant we had gone astray, or perhaps a cairn had been blown down by the strong wind and scattered by nature's elements and obliterated by sand. We had not gone very far over the rough ground as the day rapidly got hotter and our eyes burned, lips cracked and throats dried. By the time the sun set that evening, in a red ball of fire, we were very tired and weary. Thereafter the desert was to be our camp-site home. Unlike ordinary travellers, there was no need to look for a place to camp, as we had the desert all to ourselves. The outdoors became our living room. To save every minute of daylight, setting up camp became more streamlined and to overcome the space and weight problem, simply meant having less and less things to carry. A nearby bush would serve as a clothes hanger for the night, but I don't remember whose idea it was to hang stuff on them, for those 'handy little branches' happened to have very tenacious multithorned twigs which embedded themselves into our clothing. It took us a long time the next morning and some very sore fingers, to pick them all out!

The next day's ride was over sandy ridges and stony grooves, just fast enough to skim along, but it hammered the motorcycle and ourselves and we suffered some trailer-wag. Then we started to descend and though the scrub gave way to soft sand, the ground reflected the full strength of the sun's heat.

Under no circumstance was it advisable to ride into an oasis after dark and in the quiet at night, for there was no public lighting to make the occupants aware of our presence, so again our day ended 'en piste' tired, hot and hungry without reaching the oasis.

In the morning, soon after starting, we came to a standstill. Apparently we had 'goofed' our estimate of fuel for this stage of the journey, by not allowing extra for low-gear riding, unintended route diversions to avoid rocks and sand drifts, wheel-spin and the cooking stove. We had run out of petrol! Then, like a fairy tale about a princess in distress, came instant surprise and a happy ending!

The last North-bound vehicle to leave Ghardaia for three days, happened to come along. We saw dust rising in the distance. "No... its nothing". "... Yes,.. something is coming this way !"

A heavy duty desert truck stopped, as the code of courtesy prevailed in barren country, and the two Frenchmen exchanged greetings and route information. They carried a good safety margin of supplies and kindly gave us a few litres of fuel to reach Ghardaia oasis. The driver, speaking in French and turning a hand outward toward the ocean of sand, warned us, "This region is better than south of Ghardaia", to which his colleague added, "when you reach the oasis....", as we understood him to say ".. be wise, turn back!". With this advice, they drove off to make the most of the daylight - but on no account would we take his advice and turn back.

Ghardaia

Ghardaia was the largest of several small settlements on islands in the dried up river beds or *wadis*. We saw camel tracks and followed them to the main one which was the wireless outpost on the threshold of the desert. An Arab wearing loose white robes and a European jacket with red fez, was our helpful guide and interpreter, speaking the local Hausa tongue at stalls in the market place. He also restrained little boys who crowded around us shouting "Peniplees - peniplees", a familiar plea of native youngsters anywhere.

All travellers reaching an oasis in French colonial Sahara must report to the Captain of the region, in accordance with the Breakdown Contract, to show safe arrival. So our guide took us to the military barracks to report to the Captain. The hotel here had bed and bedding with sheets; food was available, though expensive. Alternatively, the Rest Shelter was the usual type of mud structure with open archways between rooms and square holes in the walls for windows. To conserve our funds, we set up our own housekeeping. Water which came from the well, several hundred feet away, was plentiful and was carried in by a native for the tip of a *sou* or two.

The Place de Djemaa market had stalls selling dates and other edibles, all settled on by swarms of flies, cleared away by hand-waving to get a glimpse of what was for sale beneath. No sooner had the flies been swept away, than immediately everything was covered again, thick black with flies. Arab merchants had chicken and eggs for sale, but camel or goat milk at other stalls, although fresh was likely to be contaminated by Malta Fever and likewise the water, had always to be boiled. In spite of their low grade fare we were eager to go on and wandered around the place looking for rations to buy. It would have taken another day to visit the Holy City of Beni-Iaguen where after sunset, only Moslems enter, or the Jewish district and ancient monasteries, but our journey was not meant to be a sight-seeing tour. In camp at the rest shelter, in the changing light of dusk when a black thread could no longer be distinguished from a white one, we heard again the Cantor chanting his lament announcing the time for Moslem prayer.

The Captain at Ghardaia greeted us with a serious face when we applied for permission to cross the Sahara. "C'est impossible pour vous avec une motorcyclette", he said firmly and for a moment it seemed further progress was after all to be denied us. "Beyond here," we understood him to say in French, in the same way we had already heard so many times before, "it is much too hazardous". We showed him the permit issued by the Société Algérienne des Transport Tropicaux (SATT) in Algiers, with a feeling of self-confidence that came from experience in dealing with officials. There was no customs formality and no objection to carrying fire-arms, but considerable trouble getting ourselves passed this deadlock. The next oasis and wireless outpost at El Golea, *(now known as El Meniaa)*, was two hundred miles into the desert. As things turned out, the Captain made a handicap arrangement with SATT for a mutual arrival time, so we would have to leave here three days ahead of the next vehicle scheduled to go through the region. The SATT desert-equipped bus was due to depart from here in four days, so on handicap, this did not give us much time to get ready. Consent to proceed was not too stringent to comply with: we must carry five gallons (20 litres) of water and ten gallons (40 litres) of fuel.

Furthermore, El Golea would be notified by wireless of the time of our departure from here and in the event of our non-arrival at El Golea, within a stipulated five day allowance, our breakdown contract would be imposed. The search would only be in the vicinity of the route and rescue charged as per contract at four francs per kilometre, each way. An oil company had established a complete refuelling arrangement across the Sahara, so fuel could be obtained at each oasis, unless several big vehicles or a convoy had recently refuelled and taken the last drop. Our trailer and sidecar locker carried food, tools, spare parts, clothes, camping equipment, camera, maps and documents. The weight of these put a strain on every nut and bolt, but after a good night's rest, we were well prepared to grapple with the first leg of the Sahara.

Florence Blenkiron breaking camp South of the Atlas Mountatins

Desert nomads in the Sahara

The Sahara
Ghardaia To El Golea

We left Ghardaia in the evening after the heat of day had subsided, to reach the next wireless outpost on the oasis of El Golea, a hundred and ninety-three miles south. We had the intention of riding all night to be sure of having time in hand and be ahead of the game when the Trans-Saharan breakdown contract was due to be put into effect. The last rays of the setting sun bid us farewell like a parting *salaam*. As we left, a camel caravan was approaching, hoping to reach Ghardaia before dark. Our route was along ground that had been rippled by other vehicles.

After dark, our headlight illuminated the side of each ripple, casting black shadows on the side of the next groove making it look like black-and-white stripes along the ground, about ten inches apart. It was never ending. The ripples caused everything on the motorcycle to shake loose and somewhere along the track we lost one of the sidecar connecting nuts and bolts. Something had also jammed inside the sidecar, locking the door to the hatch under which our tools were stored. There were no Saharan garages, so Blenk, not being at all sentimental about being so brutal to our steed, more precious to us than a King's ransom, used a rock to break open the locker door. We used a bolt, washer and nut taken from a less vital place to fix the sidecar connector. As everything had now been taken out of the locker and with the Primus stove handy, we ended the remaining hours of the night with a snack and a short sleep. Cheerfully, Blenk asked me, "Wal, what would you like for supper?", but before I could say anything, she handed me a bread and jam sandwich saying, "here's your ration - it's a worthwhile expedition".

Dawn cast light over the landscape that had shaken us up so much, showing the extent of the rocks and sand-drifts which the darkness had concealed from us. We repacked everything with military precision and know-how, ready to steal a march on sunrise and ride off before the heat of day ... and the flies.

When preparing for this venture many months ago, a well-wisher advised us to carry a roll of wire mesh to lay over deep sand where we were likely to get stuck. The idea seemed feasible since it was not heavy and could hang over the side, out of the way. As the day wore on, exasperated by pushing us out of soft sand drifts so often and seeing the huge sea of sand all around us, Blenk thought it was time to use the wire mesh. Crawling on hands and knees, she rolled it across one of those sand-drifts. I waited to ride over it, but as if in a cartoon, the springy mesh rolled itself up again. She turned around on all-fours, only for the other end to do the same thing. She finally stood up because I was laughing so much watching her trying to make it flat! We left it there to bury itself in the sand as the idea didn't work.

The piercing Saharan wind blew on one side of us. We swapped seats, without stopping, to sit backwards in the sidecar to expose our other side to the chill wind. Doing this circus performance without an audience, determined us not to give up, no matter how bad the conditions. They told us the going was not good - this surely was an under-statement. Only 24 hours from Ghardaia, all trace of the track was obliterated, but small rocks and huge stones deliberately placed in a long straight line, presumably indicated the direction to follow. It took two attempts to grapple with one unclear patch and careful not to make another mistake, we checked again to be sure, since the breakdown contract's search and rescue policy was only along the regular route. We then steered in the direction indicated, bouncing crevice to crevice between rocks and rushing across the sand-drifts. There was an everlasting horizon of wind-swept and flat-topped sand dunes. The sand drifts became longer, softer, wider and deeper and precious time was lost getting ourselves unstuck. Further south, another perfectly straight line of rocks, as big as boulders to withstand the elements, were presumably placed here to prevent us being misled by camel spore and indicated to us that we should follow that direction, so thankfully, we were after all on the right track.

Protruding through the sand, here and there, were dark patches of hard ground. Both of us, either riding on the Panther or in the sidecar, keenly looked out for these hard patches for firm traction and to avoid the powder like soft spots as well as stopping us dropping into and getting stuck in an indiscernible crevice. We ended up criss crossing the desert; "...this way ... go on ... straight ahead ... over there ... that way," steering a course that would have broken a snake's back.

In Algiers, at the start of our journey at 10 o'clock that morning, I said it would be the last occasion clocks and split seconds would be of any concern to us. However, 'time' spent in the Sahara was very important and is measured not by clock, but by water. If the motorcycle broke down, or maybe we were tired and laid on the ground to rest or bide our time on what the Arabs call 'God's Carpet', it would conserve fuel, but would not conserve water. In the land of the desert dwellers, we had not seen a sign of life for days - except flies. Nearer El Golea oasis, we saw goat-skin tents and a settlement of nomads. A Bedouin pointed in the direction of the outpost to guide us, but we disputed it. "It can't be right," Blenk commented, "that way is not fit for a camel".

El Golea

Pleased with being ahead of the break-down contract, the SATT desert vehicle from Ghardaia, travelling in a cloud of dust, caught up with us where we had become stuck in a sand-drift, so passengers were able to help us through another bad patch before they went on ahead. Just short of its destination, the bus stopped with a minor mechanical problem, so we caught up with it. The driver scribbled a note in French for us to give to the Captain of the El Golea region. We rode ahead of the bus, exalted at being courier for the SATT company and continued through the archway in the mud wall surrounding the Fort, delivering the bus driver's message to the Captain. He was very amused, not at the information, but by our tortoise and hare chase to the oasis.

El Golea was a heavenly place, like some Garden of Eden or Emerald Isle. In the midst of hundreds of miles of barren sand, an artesian well forced fresh spring water under pressure from deep underground to ripple on the surface.

In the U-shaped patio near the post office and wireless station, around white stucco buildings of Moorish style, were date palms, colourful flowers and singing birds. Camp was a day-dreamer's paradise. A friendly Arab youth attached himself to our camp-site and ran all our errands. Baki looked after our possessions when we strayed away and proved himself to be a good little shopper speaking French, as well as Arabic, at stalls in the market place. Baki looked about fourteen years old and said he needed money as he was soon to be married. "If you want me to buy you something," he said "I am ready to do so - if not, please let me go". Seventy-five centimes was a fair price for his services and Baki vanished as mysteriously as he had appeared.

A French couple wintering at the oasis by way of camel caravan, had rented a dwelling and invited us to stay with them for the night, treating us lavishly, serving an evening meal of lentil soup, camel meat and fresh-grown vegetables, gateaux, coffee and liqueur. I will never forget the friendliness of French, Arab natives and nomads alike in these out of the way places. This was New Year's Eve and we had a happy and enjoyable time.

Today was New Year Day, 1st January, 1935. That evening the Post-master/ wireless operator invited us to his house. In the chill of nightfall he wore a black scarlet-lined cloak that flashed different colours as he walked. Later, he turned on the wireless for us to hear the BBC and to listen to the news from home in English. The chimes of 'Big Ben' - the knell of the time-honoured London clock, struck a contrast between there and here, bringing home to me, something more clear than the period of time. In my mind I could picture the crowds, culture, cuisine, concrete and folk in their hum-drum jobs at home, secure in a challenging world, at a time in my life when the standard set for women was regulated by those who themselves did not live by them. I would rather grapple with the sands of the Sahara than the sands of contemporary society.

The next day, we walked back to the barracks to seek from the Captain his consent to ride the next two hundred and fifty miles into the desert to the In-Salah oasis and wireless outpost.

He was friendly, but firm, just like the other French Foreign Legionnaires in his staff. Each of them said we should not attempt going any further south or try to reach the next oasis. We listened to their warning. The Captain went on to explain again, "... shifting sands, worse than north of El Golea, had completely obliterated some of the stacked-up heaps of stone markers and as far as you could see, there was nothing at all to mark the direction to follow". He described the Tademait Plateau, about half way to In-Salah, as a table-flat region some five hundred feet higher, being very difficult to ascend and descend. According to the available information, the region was described on our chart as "the land then falls away in terraces until the final drop of some two hundred feet into the ocean of the In-Salah sands, where south of the plateau, the highest peaks of the Hoggar Mountains rise up out of the sea of sand like other mountains elsewhere rise up over snow."

"What will you do," the Lieutenant wanted to know, "if the Hoggar Massif drifts engulf you?" I tried to make clear, in his own language, how we use the block and tackle. "When the motorcycle gets stuck in sand we use the trailer as anchor to attach the rope, pull together to drag it out", then Blenk continued in her French "... if the trailer gets stuck, we use the motorcycle as anchor to pull it out". I carried on, " ... if the worst comes to the worst, we would abandon the trailer and load only fuel, water and food into the sidecar," to which Blenk added, "... a motorcycle does not need radiator water." Together we talked on and on, with no intention of yielding to the officer's warnings and were determined to be the first to ride over the Sahara and across the African continent to Cape Town, even though we had failed to bring a compass with us!

Sometimes we could understand a little French from hearing it being repeated so many times; at other times we could not comprehend a thing, but as the conversation developed, despite new words being added to our vocabulary, while the words may have been different, the meaning was always the same. Eventually the Captain tired of hearing our appalling French and agreed that we would leave El Golea under similar conditions as before, namely five days in advance of whichever day the next SATT vehicle was due to go south, allowing us a six day handicap to reach the In-Salah oasis and wireless outpost.

The Captain of the In-Salah region, the fourth oasis along the line, would be informed by wireless of our departure from El Golea at which time the Breakdown contract would be put into effect. We prepared everything very carefully for the next treacherous part of our journey. The Panther had been serviced and we were ready. We waited a couple of days to hear when the next vehicle would depart southwards and then left El Golea on handicap. Our letters and reports from here would reach home, some day.

The In Salah Sands
El Golea To In Salah

In the early morning sunshine, the oriental shaped archway of the mud wall surrounding El Golea oasis, cast it's black shadow over the yellow sand as we rode out into the desert again. We had changed from our European winter breeches, boots and overcoats into a lightweight tropical outfit, safari shirts with spine-pads attached and lead-foil lined topee helmets, looking more like the adventurers we were. The spine pad was designed to protect us against the strong ultraviolet of the sun's rays in the torrid zone. It was a snap-on, T-shaped piece of scarlet flannel, worn outside the shirt across the shoulders and down the spine and was covered with the same material as the shirt so as not to appear like a red cross. At this time of the year, the sun's rays reach the furthest point north of the equator.

South of here, they could be most harmful. An imaginary line drawn around the earth at about this latitude passes the constellation of stars that look like a crab, Cancer. We now prepared to cross into the zone of the Tropic of Cancer. We had been warned about the peril of powder-like drifts of soft sand north and south of In-Salah that settled in enormous hollows. Our narrow tyres cut through the soft surface and we got stuck so many times that progress was like swimming in syrup; it was miserably slow. We knew the knack of extracting ourselves from our club competition and trials riding experience. The rope and tackle allowed us to move forward fifteen feet at a time. In the full heat of mid-day, our dry throats were consuming too much of our water ration and with the engine revving in low gear, we were also using valuable fuel. This section of the Sahara was rapidly taking up the time allowance in our breakdown contract - even so, we made as much progress as we could until sun set, when we made camp for the night.

The sun rose from behind the sand dunes and revealed a 360^0 panorama of barrenness with such a feeling of space, we knew we were deep in the desert. Like the guides for the camel caravans who know their route, we tried to spot and avoid the more treacherous places. When all the wheels sank into deep soft sand, we were in real trouble - at least for a while, though perhaps for hours or even days. During the hottest summer months, the temperature rose to about 120°F and the ground became almost too hot to stand on. Only a few camel caravans travelled at this time of year, but no motor vehicles would for all the wireless outposts were closed. Hopefully by then, we would be elsewhere. We laid underneath the trailer in the small oblong shadow cast by the sun, for shelter from the mid-day sun's heat in one of the hottest places on earth. When the sun passed overhead we got ourselves moving again.

31

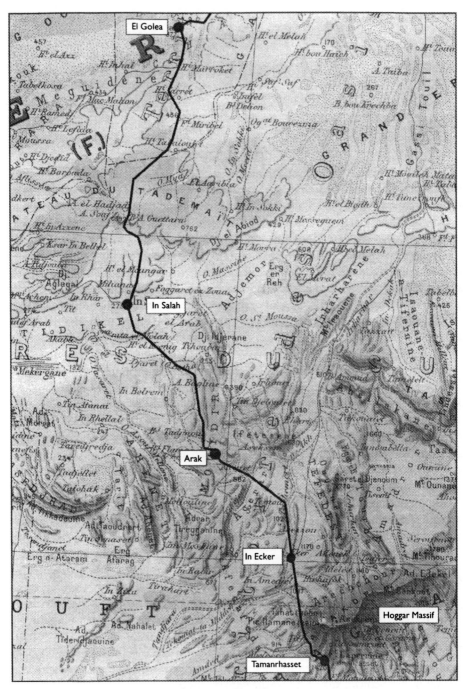

El Golea to Tamanrhasset

The ground was so hot that abnormal air density changed the direction of light through the atmosphere with such a strange effect that we saw a mirage. Refracted light-rays showed displaced images of a flowing stream of water and graceful palm trees, so much so that it appeared as if a settlement was not far away. Frequently seen and unmistakably realistic, but none was there. A mirage is an amazing spectacle, but we knew better than to be misled by the optical illusion.

A slight technical hitch

The U-coupling broke from the strain of towing the trailer. Reversing the hitch was alright, but doubled the load on the other half of the hook and after a while it also broke. The only help was about two hundred miles back or a hundred and fifty miles further on. This particular soft, sandy area was apparently a notorious disaster spot that had defeated other unfortunate travellers. As we looked around we could see not far away a wrecked car of some sort protruding out of the sand. I walked, or rather ploughed my feet, through the sand over to where the heap had been abandoned and to my joy I saw that the lugs were all that remained on it. They were welded to the chassis, but on the underside, some were bolted on, and by using the adjustable wrench one of them came off.

When our venture was being planned, well before we used the metric system, we did not realise our Whitworth gauge tools would not fit metric nuts and bolts and of course our one inch diameter linkage-pin would not go through the two centimetre lug hole from the wrecked car. Without the help of a vice or anything else to hold the lug, Blenk used the rat-tail file to enlarge the diameter of the hole while I used a flat file to reduce the diameter of our linkage-pin. After a while we changed over, Blenk filed the pin and I filed the lug-hole. We had almost a quarter of an inch to file off between us to get the two parts to fit. It got dark and still the pin and the lug would not fit together. The night wind felt strong, but there were no trees or street corners or anything but our own equipment to make it whine. Suddenly Blenk let out a yell. "Oo, oo, oh!" I thought she had been bitten by something or had hurt herself, but she had just remembered a gift from the Christmas party in Algiers! "We've got some Cognac!"

The sun woke us. Tools were scattered all around and Blenk was using the flat file, holding the lug-hole piece and I had the rat-tail file with the oversize connecting pin! I grumbled, "did you say Cognac would give us staying power or power to stay ?" We pulled ourselves together and finished the job in daylight, coupled up the trailer and went on.

Tademait Plateau

The ascent to the Tademait Plateau was one incline after another, steep and arduous just as the Captain at El Golea had told us, but when up there on hard ground, the block and tackle was no longer needed and was stowed away. Every half kilometre, a big piled up heap of stones could be clearly seen in the distance, marking the direction to follow. Although some had tumbled down, their scattered pieces served their purpose. The flat and badly corrugated stony ground went on for about a hundred miles without a bulwark or cranny for refuge. At one stage, we could actually see the curvature of the earth. Shaken up by the corrugations along the Tademait Plateau, we seldom spoke to each other, but often changed seats from saddle to sidecar, uncertain whether or where we would stop to rest. In the strong wind the 'Primus' stove did not work very well despite a makeshift screen around it, so the extent of cooking our evening meal was simply to heat soup or make tea, since water had to be boiled anyway.

Brilliant full-moonlight that night, shining through clear skies, was bright enough to read or write. It illuminated our surroundings. Standing beside me was a big black thing that suddenly moved and scared me - it was only my own shadow.

Hour after hour of sheer monotony, thumping over grooves in the track, the only compensation we had was the edifying experience of having endured riding across the Tademait Plateau. This plateau surely must be the bleakest place on earth to find one's soul, if nothing else.

The steep gradient down the plateau was in rocky stages, dropping down about 1,500 ft to a lower altitude. Trying not to slide sideways caused some anxious moments as we descended again into a sea of soft sand. Our wheels sank into powder like sand sending up clouds of fine dust which fell down over everything, finding its way inside the sidecar and all over the trailer and ourselves. We had to unpack the block and tackle again and do more rope-pulling to drag the motorcycle out by means of the trailer and vice versa. Sometimes we leaned shoulder-to-shoulder on each other to form a tripod with the motorcycle, so one arm each lifted the rear wheel enough for a spare foot to kick rock and hard stuff underneath for traction. That worked better than the wire mesh. The advantage of a motorcycle when wedged in, was that it could be lifted out.

Big man-made heaps of rocks, a kilometre apart which marked the direction to follow, had tumbled to the ground. In some places of this worsening In-Salah quagmire, only sand covered humps along the ground gave us a clue as to the direction. Thankfully we had not gone astray and were still going in the right direction. We soon began to realise the magnitude and severity of the Sahara desert. We were a thousand miles from Algiers, barely half way across, but were not yet licked. Perhaps there was a reason why everyone had said we would not succeed in getting across.

Daylight faded and supper was as usual a survival fare of plain tea, stale bread and dates. The evening was enriched by the clear upper atmosphere free from air pollution and seeing stars that did not twinkle. The entire Heaven appeared magnificently dimensional. The wind was blowing a miniature sand-storm a few inches above the ground covering all trace of our own track.

Moisture in the descending cool night air settled on the soft powder-like sand making the fine grains stick together. Early in the morning the surface was more firm until the sun heated the ground, evaporated the dew and made the sand soft treacherous again. Brilliant sunlight shone down from a cloudless blue sky and dazzling reflection came up from the sand beneath us, making the glare so intense that rocks cast no shadow. The dark wrap-around eye shields we were wearing made it very difficult to see clearly the best path to pick as we thrust our way along, now and again bumping into unseen outcrops but fortunately without damage. We steered as directly southward as possible winding a path between rocky outcrop and deep sand drifts. These conditions played havoc with tyres, fuel allowance, water rations and the breakdown contract time allowance. After four days we seemed to be heading towards the In Salah oasis and the Fort would be somewhere not 'far away'.

In this part of the world it rains about every four to six years. Just a few days before we came along, as luck would have it, a strong wind had blown rain cloud over the region and a shower made sand around here more firm than usual. At last, in the distance, we saw palm trees clinging to the oasis and then the tall wireless masts of In-Salah came into view, standing up black against the blue sky. It was a truly welcome sight.

Camel train in the Sahara, Blenk watching

Dragging the trailer out of the sand

Desert oasis

Life In The Oasis
In Salah

At the gateway in the mud wall surrounding In Salah Fort and wireless outpost, soldiers of the French Foreign Legion sprang to attention with transfixed eyes - instead of fixed bayonets - and beckoned us forward. But we had got stuck again in the sand and were unable to obey their command. Plenty of willing hands appeared and helped push us along a few feet to the entrance of a mud building. Within the compound a solitary Arab woman, carrying an earthenware vessel balanced on her head, walked across as a picture of elegance. A few real life Tuaregs (pronounced 'twa-regs') were resting in a shady corner and everyone else at this mid-day, was out of sight.

A regiment of the French Foreign Legion was stationed at each oasis, maintaining wireless communication and upholding law and order among the tribes or anyone else causing a disturbance from one end of the Sahara to the other.

A bugle call, like a musical alarm clock, pierced the air as far out as the outlying nomad camps, indicating the time of day: Reveille, Mid-day (siesta), or 'Taps'. The Legionnaire who sounded this noon call gave a rousing fanfare in full tune and hearty rhythm, he was certainly a musician. The Captain, a tall, blond and smartly uniformed Legionnaire came from his den to acknowledge our safe arrival. "Well - well!" it sounded like, "I never expected you to arrive so soon, or at all - when El Golea said you were coming by motorcycle!". He spoke a little English and kindly offered us shelter, without charge, in the traveller's rest hut.

The shelter was quite clean and comfortable. Open archways separated four compartments each furnished with two trestle beds and white sheets, two chairs and a wooden crate that served as a table on which there were two candles, a ten-litre jug of water and a wash bowl. In this barrack-like setting, relieved of the strain from struggling against sand and time apportioned by the breakdown contract, everything we possessed was unloaded from the sidecar and trailer and tipped on the earth floor for a grand tidy up and house-cleaning. Veiled Tuaregs ended their day as they walked past towards their goat skin tents, camped near a fertile place. Leading a nomadic life herding camels, sheep or goats, they roamed the surrounding scrub land. I felt we had something in common with these nomads as we moved along from place to place, not having a fixed abode. The glorious desert sunset turned to dusk and a never to be forgotten Sahara night. In the sky we saw the spectacle of the Constellation of the Southern Cross. The armed guard by the gate stood at ease, scarcely moving and looked more dignified as darkness fell upon them. Reminiscent of my childhood days holding a candle on my way upstairs to bed, I lighted one of these candles and laid down on this cot thinking of the books about Africa that I could reach along the lower shelves in the library; they seemed to come alive like a dream come true.

In the morning we had nothing for breakfast except stale bread and dates, but when we tipped everything out of the trailer, the Christmas pudding, tossed into the sidecar by a well-wisher when we left London (almost a month ago), made it's appearance. In a Moslem country, without Christmas decorations, we performed a little foolery and ceremonial dance around the pudding singing *'For the sake of Auld Lang Syne'*. Our only audience were some ants - unfortunately the ants had got into the pudding! Blenk exclaimed meaningfully, "We are not going to bring the pudding all this way and not eat it!'. Since the ants were the same colour as the pudding, we kept our eyes peeled for anything that moved, and picked the ants out for entertainment.

When walking to the market place, we stood awhile at the opening of a goat skin tent. Tuaregs inside the tent were unperturbed by us strangers. On the contrary, by the gesture of a hand we were able to meet them and from the fragrance it was clear they were brewing green tea - far more preferable where water has a high salt content. The pale flame of their fire to boil the water was kindled from a small bunch of twigs. After the third tiny but sweetest cup of brew, it was customary for a visitor to depart. The market place was like I imagined it to be. Tuareg men and women sat on mats laid on the ground. Above them were mats mounted on poles for shade. Around them were spread their wares for sale and all around were French, Arab and Huasa stalls, together with camels, goats and chickens ... and flies. We wanted to buy some muslin to cover our food from flies and came to a stall selling fabrics. The merchant measured a length of material just the same way as I remembered the old English draper did, by holding one end to his nose and cutting off a length (a metre or yard) at the full extent of his arm. We wandered around the market to find necessities for the next hazardous part of our journey to the outpost of Tamanrhasset in the Hoggar Mountains.

Our problem was trailer space and overall weight. The chosen lifestyle of adventurers, living in want, was more gratifying to me than a 'life of Riley', but the compromise was not easy to balance and know just how much was enough. Dates were sold by the handful. Butter was unobtainable in this heat and for some time now we had been used to not having any. Canned milk was better than fresh goat milk, which always had to be boiled since it was likely to be contaminated with Malta Fever, a febrile disease which first made its appearance in Malta.

A leather worker had made a saddle and we watched a silver smith puffing a small fire with hand-made bellows of wood slats and goat skin, while shaping a Tuareg (Southern) Cross from a big five-franc silver coin - a beautiful souvenir, that I wanted very much, but we had neither money nor space to spare for anything at all unless absolutely necessary for the next part of our journey. The market had 'free trade' in the truest sense, which meant French currency - cash, no receipt, no tax or sometimes, no money at all as they simply exchanged goods between themselves. Merchants shouted their wares to attract attention to the stall and then haggled with a prospect to make a deal. We soon found out there was no set price for anything!

Almost everything for human existence in the Sahara was transported by camel caravan, and that being so they were vulnerable to attack. So beside soldiers of the French Foreign Legion, both Arab and Tuareg caravan guides had their own security guards for protection. Merchandise from one oasis to the next was carried along their own camel tracks travelling at night when it was cool, guided by the stars. They had their drinking water in porous goat skin bags so that slight evaporation kept it cooler, which gave us the idea that we should do it the same way, for our water in the trailer was quite hot. In the desert, *kel*, is the word for people whose tribes bear geographical place names to identify themselves with the region they call their homeland. This was the Ajjer region of the Sahara and here was a tribe of the Kel Ajjer people. The veil in Tuareg language is *tagilmus* and as the word for people is kel, so they call themselves Kel Tagilmus, 'People of the Veil'.

Their veil is a long narrow strip of cloth wrapped around the head several times leaving a narrow opening for the eyes and as it is put on, one edge hangs over the forehead to protect the eyes and folds over the mouth and chin loose enough to be able to eat. Tuareg women protect themselves from sun, wind and blown dust by use of the fringe of the robe and a shawl wrapped around a straw hat. As they are not outside the tent so much, women do not wear the veil. A veil made of fine indigo-dyed cotton is good shade in their very hot land, but when breathing against the cloth, moist air around the nostrils and mouth will filter the dust, but the indigo dye will rub off onto the skin giving them extra protection from the burning sun. This makes the Tuaregs look fearful at first sight until it is seen that this beautiful feature distinguishes them, so they are often called 'The Blue People'.

Allah - they say, needs the Sahara so mankind can retreat therein to peace and silence from the troubled world. *Allah*, they say, created the world and mankind to live in it and had two lumps of clay left - from one, He moulded the camel and from the other, a palm tree so humanity could survive. This is how the Tuareg people, a tribe of Berbers, neither Negro nor Arab, feel about their homeland.

Our three days in In-Salah, deep in the Sahara, was a wonderful experience. The Captain wanted us in his office again and we had a good idea what it would be about. Military authorities were in no hurry to give us their approval to continue or allow us into the Hoggar Mountain region, so we usually had to persist and argue our way along. The next span of more than 400 miles was the longest and most difficult of all the Sahara hurdles. One hundred miles from here, at Arak, would be sweet water, but then no more water for another 150 miles until the Well of In-Ecker.

A Legionnaire said it was impossible for a motorcycle to get through very bad sand drifts approaching the Hoggar Massif and ascend through the Gorge d'Arak at 5,000 ft, to reach the wireless outpost on the summit at the oasis of Tamanrhasset. The Captain spoke a few words in English and the rest with his hands. He was very tolerant of us speaking 'Franglais' and explained, "The south side of the mountain range is formidable with deep soft sand and heat for a distance of more than 400 square miles extending around the Peaks which themselves rise to 8000 ft (though quoted to us in kilometres) which are covered with snow". Our French vocabulary was not improving, but was good enough to persuade the Captain, who was concerned about our safety, that we would get through. With a breakdown contract time allowance adjusted to our six-day life support endurance, passage was finally approved for our continuing expedition.

The motorcycle was ready; trailer and sidecar carefully repacked and everything checked. In the cool of the night of 7th January, 1935, we started on our southward bound journey from In Salah to Tamanrhasset.

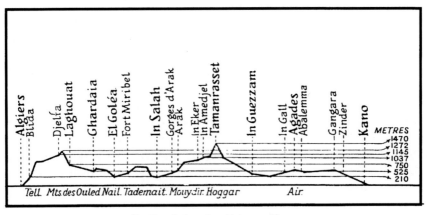

Sectional elevation Algiers to Kano

The Hoggar Massif
In Salah To Tamanrhasset

A few hours after we left, the Captain of the In-Salah region sent two Legionnaires in a desert truck to follow us and find out for themselves whether they should intervene before it was too late and avert disaster by calling a halt to our attempt to ride across the Sahara and become the first people to traverse the African continent overland to Cape Town.

After about twenty miles they caught up with us, stuck in sand pushing our motorcycle through a sand drift. They helped push in their bare feet with sand over their ankles to keep us moving and spared us precious breakdown contract time allowance and then bid us 'Adieu!' before turning their mouse-grey truck back to base, leaving us heart and soul to carry on. Powdery sand shot up into the air, high and wide, as if a compressor had blown into it to stifle and smother us. We skimmed through another drift. Every hundred feet or so, dark patches of hard mineral-looking ground protruded, but between them were troughs of soft sand. We dashed from one patch of hard ground to another until the sand-drifts between became so wide and deep that we could no longer leap-frog along unless we lightened the load. Everything was unloaded. Then in low gear, with the engine revving, by running and pushing alongside, we would drop the clutch and buck-jump aboard, as if starting a racing motorcycle without a kick-starter. Our unladen wheels skimmed over the bad places to the next dark patch of hard ground. Back-and-forth we walked to bring over all our belongings, piece-by-piece and reload, careful to leave nothing behind. Blenk voiced: "You know, we are doing this of our own accord?" "Yes," I said, "but this is a hiking trip more that a motorcycle trip". I don't remember how many times we did this along the desolate stretch of more than 250 miles between In-Salah and Arak, on the way to Tamanrhasset, but in spite of hardship, we were free to put our civil liberty into practice in a most adventurous way.

In my schoolbook, the map of Algeria was an empty space and in the minds of many people, they had only a vague impression about the Sahara desert. Certainly no pictures or words written or spoken truly describe this unterrestrial-like place except perhaps by comparison with discoveries about the surface of another planet. When NASA (North American Space Agency) sent the *Viking I* and *Viking II* spaceships to look at Mars, the satellites took pictures and sent them back to earth, so mankind could have a look at the planet next to us. Pictures received on earth very much resembled the Sahara landscape showing what looked like stones, boulders and dunes of various size. There were places where liquid seemed to have been part of a vast river system shaping the outline of islands, yet nowhere was there any water. There was reason to believe the Mars landscape had been moulded by the effects of shifting dunes, flowing liquid and dried up river beds just like those all around us here in the Sahara desert, in which queer outcrops of rock, in dried up river beds called *wadis*, could be recognised. NASA then ventured to say the pictures of Mars might very well have been taken in the Sahara and that a camel caravan would not have looked out of place.

When we actually did see a camel caravan pass by, it was a heart-throbbing sight. However, we did have air to breath, but the Mars gravity would have suited us better. Riding over this Mars-like terrain we could see the detailed surface of our planet at closer range from astride our motorcycle than would be possible any other way except by camel. In spite of it's harshness, the Sahara, by nature, is endowed with it's own austere beauty. As we penetrated deeper into this unearthly place our motorcycle was more than something tangible made of metal and rubber, but having an empathy like a living soul possessed of feeling - it was also quite companionable. It was our home. Our exploit was not intended to be a geographical expedition, nor did we pretend to be geologists, photographers or journalists, nor under the circumstances, have time to write many notations bout people and places. Blenk and I, with a bit of true-life reality, were simply going to see Africa.

The next time the wheels sank in sand, at about 5,000 ft altitude, we were too tired to go any further and stopped to camp. Time, the fourth dimension, will wait for no one and by now we had spent two days of the breakdown contract time allowance.

January was not usually the month for sand storms, which can be dangerous, especially where there is no shelter. If a sudden gust of wind came along and lifted the top layer of fine sand much higher, already swirling a few inches above the ground, it would blot out the sun. It would be dark enough for us to be unable to see above our heads and would cover us over. A camel has adapted to desert conditions very well and can survive a sand storm. A camel treads on it's feet or pads, as big as a saucer, without sinking in the sand. Long legs carry it's body above the hottest air radiated from the ground and the long neck and raised head, reach above the average level of a sand storm allowing the camel to see and breath air relatively clear of sand. When the warm wind changes and blows from the south, it can lift a certain weight of fine-grain sand which forms the perilous drifts against the Massif. It gets carried in the air higher and higher, far away across the Mediterranean sea and reaches the tops the Alps, coating the snow on those mountains with a yellow deposit, and dusting cars in those little Swiss towns. A notorious sand storm around El Golea, several years after we came through, killed people, camels and as many as fifteen hundred goats and two thousand sheep.

At low altitude, dangerous areas of sand settle in hollows like puddles of oil floating on water. Although not perceptibly moving, they are 'shifting sands'. This entire area of moving sand mass is called an *Erg*. El Golea was in the Grand Erg Occidental and luckily, after a very rare rainfall, we managed to get across. Rocky places called *Hammadas* such as the Tademait Plateau north of In-Salah, already well behind us, separate the eastern and western Ergs. Part of the western Erg still to be negotiated, lay before Tamanrhasset. Sand between mountain and plateau cover only part of the enormous desert.

Since the first mission by the French Government barely eighty years before us, large areas of the Sahara remained un-surveyed. Tuaregs and desert guides know the skyline. There are names for well-defined shapes. 'Star dunes' are firm ridges of rock and sand that serve as dependable landmarks. Star dunes on one occasion gave us our bearings from near here. When off course or diverting to try and get through by taking the line of least resistance, we went back to re-sight the skyline and try again to sight another cairn marker. Sand dunes are changeable. Wind will change the undulating shape and position of sand dunes like the tide does the ocean waves, but not the panorama as a whole. The formation of sand dunes, like ocean waves, have a semblance of order. I had sailed the Atlantic by ship and thought of the analogy between rolling ocean breakers and sand dunes. If the ocean swell and billowing water waves could for an instant be held motionless - then by a quirk of imagination, they would be transformed into sand and a similar pattern would emerge. The Tuareg guides read the sand like mariners read the water, and they call it 'the sea without water', and their camels, 'ships of the desert'.

A legionnaire at In-Salah had sketched a diagram of the outline of star dunes on the horizon to warn us to be on the look-out for an especially bad area and change course to avoid it. After dark we sank deep in a soft place. Our headlight probed into an endless expanse of sand, but too tired for any more pulling and pushing, we pitched tent and slept until dawn so we could see our way more clearly, before the sun and the flies were very bad. It may not have been a good idea after all to ride at night, unless in bright moonlight, yet in daytime we had to stop in 120°F and shelter in shade underneath the trailer.

We tried to average forty-five miles a day, or about twice the pace of a camel caravan, to keep within the time allowance of our breakdown contract. Overnight, sand-drifts piled up against us and erased our own wheel tracks. Dawn light came from the 'wrong' direction and revealed a formidable expanse of soft sand as far as we could see. Search party guides check only along the presumed route and we had gone astray! Like old-timers we took bearings, observed the tops of rigid star dunes, turned about 180° and went back a distance. "THERE!", Blenk yelled, pointing along the ground to a man-made triangle of rocks, "THIS way!", she beckoned. We stood by the three-sided arrangement of rocks and could see in the distance a cairn of marker-rocks and from that position, the horizon in every respect resembled the diagram sketched by the legionnaire as an area to be avoided. Neither of us was alert enough to have noticed it. "Who missed that?" she grunted. I shouted, pointing to hard ground, "Look there - that way - we'll be alright now", and with tongue in cheek "there can't be much more sand in the world - *du sable - du sable*", I mumbled "sand is our trouble - it is in everything, the food, the fuel - never again will I ever go to a sandy seaside" and then Blenk reminded me that Cape Town was at the seaside!

Dry desert air, unable to retain its daytime heat, rapidly drops in temperature as the sun sets, so the night feels quite chilly. The woodwork of our trailer, made in damp industrial Birmingham, had warped badly in the ever changing temperature and to keep it in shape required some amateur carpentry. The sides at least had to be kept parallel, but we hardly knew where to begin fixing it. The lid that we laid on rocked and creaked, but it would kept us high off the ground out of harm's way from ants, snakes or other creepy-crawlies and the wet weather, as we got further south. A tent was raised over it when camping, not always for privacy, but for shelter from the weather. Our sleeping bags were unrolled to enjoy the most comfortable rest. Only when really required did we use our headlight to give us light. In moonlight, especially as it was so cold, the sand looked like snow and rocks close to the 'white' ground cast weird black shadows that moved with the rotation of earth, staging their silent movie.

"The horn," I said, reaching over the handlebar to switch off the side light, "should be disconnected - whenever something touches the horn button it blasts like a lost sheep. Besides, we don't need it". "No!", Blenk argued, "it amused the Bedouins up north so let's not silence it for the Tuaregs - even if the moon falls on it!". I warned her, "Next time we scare nomads at night we might not be so lucky!", but by then she had already dozed off.

The Gorge d'Arak

The sun appeared between the star dunes. We struggled to ascend more than a thousand feet through the Gorge d'Arak towards the Hoggar Massif, the most beautiful yet harrowing climb imaginable. Morning light striking the high canyon wall of the ravine caught my eye, revealing layers of different coloured mineral deposits formed since eternity. Windswept formations, like castles in the air, surely were a geological time-piece. As our tiny vehicle climbed up very slowly through the Gorge, we felt like little beetles in a burrow. Half way through the Gorge d'Arak, we stopped and camped in an out of the way nook where no wind was blowing, nor rays of sunlight came through until overhead at midday. Close by was a small hotel that looked dwarfed at the foot of volcanic peaks.

As a formality like any other outpost, although the staff here were French civilians, we were supposed to report our safe arrival. An Arab brought us the purest water, but the price of food was very expensive. Anyway, their French bread, which was made to order, was worth waiting for. The soldiers who followed us on the way out of In Salah a few days ago and had now caught up with us, were well supplied with rations and rather than take all the food back to base had generously given us a can of butter, milk and a whole roast chicken. The innkeeper cautioned us about the danger of climbing to higher altitude explaining, in French, how fine grain sand blown by the wind heaped against the Hoggar Massif. Water, he said, but no food, would be found half way to Tamanrhasset, in about 145 miles, at the well of In-Ecker. The following morning, after an invitation to join our friends for *cafe au lait* and last minute tidings, we were allowed a revised SATT six-day time limit to reach the oasis and wireless outpost at Tamanrhasset. The few personnel stationed here gathered to see us off.

All the while we scanned the horizon for sight of another cairn-marker and gradually ascending with heavy load, we got stuck in deep sand again and again. With the breakdown contract time allowance ticking away, we were at least going in the right direction. Any feeling of something wrong with the motorcycle could not be neglected and we attended to it without delay. The tool-box was opened several times and when we stopped flies settled all over us.

In-Ecker

We reached the tiny oasis of In-Ecker. Although it was not a wireless outpost, the fact that water was here in the well made it a significant place. The abundance of water from the artesian well, raised by internal pressure, brought about a beautiful change of scenery. We saw green vegetation, pretty gardens, singing birds and the inhabitants wearing long white smocks, resembling Biblical figures. Flies were literally a 'fly in the face' for this pretty place. An Arab made us bread to eke out our ration from home-grown mealie flour, by the age-old method of baking in a sand-oven.

Their time intervals were: dawn, noon (sun overhead) and dusk. One o'clock meant 'noon and wait a little', while two o'clock was 'noon and wait a little longer'. Exactly one month to the day since we left London on December 11th, with it's timetables, tide tables and winter fog, we slept under the sky bursting with stars which sent to earth their various intensities of light, like some kind of inter-celestial communication. I wish we could have spent more time here to become better acquainted with life on this tiny Saharan refuge.

The next day, at some uncertain time and place, we crossed the Tropic of Cancer into the torrid zone and ascended another *Hammada*, or stony plateau, where there were many small volcanic pinnacles. All day we rode over virgin ground at about fifteen miles an hour, admiring the austere beauty without having another flat tyre or any other mechanical problem. As we came off the Plateau we descended into soft sand near Mt Tahat, the highest peak at 9,530 ft and often snow-capped. As the innkeeper at Arak had warned us, drifts of soft sand were heaped up at the foot of the mountain.

One night as we changed places from saddle to sidecar without stopping, a blanket slipped overboard touching the horn button. "HONK" went the horn. I shouted, "I've dropped the blanket". Blenk stopped. Nomad encampments were usually near an oasis, but a tribe nearby was disturbed by noise. As I walked back looking down along the ground to find our beige coloured blanket, which was hard to see in the dark as it lay on the sandy ground, I eventually found it and looking up, saw we were silently surrounded by veiled Kel Ajjer Tuaregs, who had made no sound. They were on friendly terms and we had no reason to be afraid of them. Tuareg people have lived in the Hoggar Mountain region since the distant past and it is said they are not religious, but like some people they believe spirits are in Heaven and on earth.

They see the stars as 'eyes' watching to keep them to their ancestral past and the noises they hear are the spirits talking. These Tuaregs were from the settlement of Tit, a little-known habitat, a few miles north of Tamanrhasset, which means 'eye' in the sense that 'springs are the earth's eyes'. Later we came to the settlement of Tit where their goat skin tents, nestled into the rocky landscape, conveyed the lifestyle of Tuareg desert dwellers. We stopped to see them and hoped to buy some of their produce and obtain fresh goat milk. Soon we were again surrounded by quaint tribe-people who had never seen a motorcycle before. They watched us as we prepared to camp and squatted around with the same curiosity as the Bedouins in the north. The Primus stove roared loudly as it boiled our water, but in sunlight the flame was not visible. A staid Tuareg in the group came close to convince himself that it was hot and had boiled the water. While the stove was still bellowing away, he passed his case-hardened foot, able to tread on burning hot sand, across the invisible flame. Still puzzled he beckoned another and together they stared at the device. It would have taken until darkness for them to actually see the flame and to believe there could be fire without smoke.

We retired inside the tent over the trailer and settled down to a good night's sleep leaving the prying-eyed Tuaregs squatting on their haunches. If we had come upon a tribe like the feared Bedouin in the north, some of whom were fugitives who regarded the looting of caravans and travellers for weapons as part of their occupation, it would be prudent not to show them our guns, a line of reasoning we followed with the Tuareg. However we felt there was no reason to be jittery about them, but if they intended to harm us, it was as well they did it while we slept.

At daybreak, the crackling of burning twigs made us wonder if they had set us on fire with evil intention and we fearfully peeped out of the tent. We dressed in turn as there was not enough room inside to do otherwise and we stepped outside. A wild-looking audience, curious as cats, with some wearing the *burnoose*, a hooded cloak, stared at us. They may have been there all night gathered around a warming fire. A friendly Tuareg woman came forward to offer us a bowl of goat milk and some dates, so any fear we may have had about them was quite unjustified.

To have been able to meet these fascinating people was another worthwhile experience. In some places in the peaks, water could be found though only the Kel Ajjar people and those desert guides knew where to look. Tales are told of people who perished quite near water, but unable to find it. But we knew better than to go tramping around or do anything we were not very careful about. We rested in readiness for a spooky moonlight night ride to the summit.

The Hoggar Massif

Along the way on each side of the twisty track were many smaller pinnacles which lined the direction to follow and every one of them cast its own peculiarly shaped black shadow upon the ground, gradually changing profile with the rotation of the earth. They presented a pageant of 'moon-dials' for mile after mile, like a musical composition with variations of the same theme. The Tuareg legend claims that no one may climb the peak named Garet el Djenoun, east of Arak, without consent of Jenoun, the Spirit that haunts the Hoggar Mountains. It transpired that my own Vagabond Spirit was in company with Jenoun Spirit, and together with the Spirit of Allah, they were lifted by the wind like floating sand grains, to rendezvous at the summit of the Garet el Djenoun, their intention being to enlighten my Vagabond Spirit about how to go to Heaven - rather than how the Heavens go.

Prehistoric settlements discovered in the Tassili-n-Ajjer plateau, north of the Hoggar Mountains, have artwork on the rock face showing forms of animals and paintings of human figures, believed to be 7,000 years old, proving the existence of a civilisation that once lived here when the Sahara was a fertile place. Wide horizontal seams of different rock formation stretched for miles, exposing mineral geology which chronicled the earth's make-up, dating back millions of years. Since the beginning of time, heaps of lava called Massifs piled up. The Hoggar and Tassili have been lashed with sand-laden wind and at times heavy rainfall, blasting the lava deposits and beating the Massif into all sorts of fantastic shapes. Flat-topped windswept dunes, buttes resembling domes, pyramids and black cones, many carved out, formed canyons and caves where ancient people once lived. There are of course, some remarkable geological wonders in other parts of the world, though I never expected anything like this in the Sahara.

As we approached Tamanrhasset, the highest part of the desert and a cross-roads for camel caravans, the most amazing sight of all happened to be the last stretch. Our 'Grand Finale', so-to-speak, was the spectacle of handiwork by both man and nature. It was the culmination of six days rugged ride. Nestled at the foot of the high volcanic pinnacles of the Hoggar Massif, terrific sized boulders and date palms, were native handmade grandiloquent columns, like Totem poles, which formed a majestic colonnade that neither tribal wars nor weather had yet undone. We rode our motorcycle on firm ground alongside these stately pillars, going slowly like a Chieftain on his camel, or a King on his throne, as though part of some royal procession.

Nothing stirred. We entered this silent settlement of the living with a ghostly feeling as though we had come to a lost city of the past - it was simply siesta time!

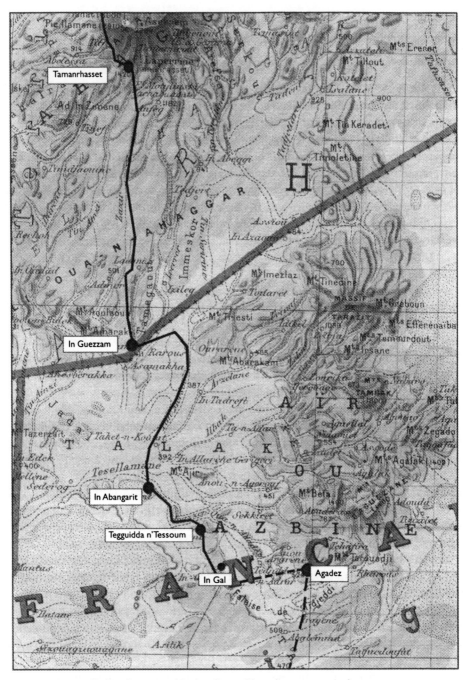

Tamanrhasset to Agadez. Dotted line shows presumed route.

Peeks In The Peaks
Tamanrhasset To In Guezzam

The staccato noise of our motorcycle, which by now had lost its silencer, aroused drowsy folk from their midday siesta as we rolled to a standstill in Tamanrhasset. Arabs and Tuaregs gathered around us to see the strangers riding a horse-on-wheels. This was the first motorcycle to reach here - they had never seen one before. Being tired and weary after six days hard riding for 250 miles and the climb up here, only just within our breakdown contract limit, we wanted to report to the Captain of this region as soon as possible. A Frenchman inside the mud building came from behind a coloured bead-curtain and we asked him the usual question, "Where is the Captain, please ?" Speaking slowly in French, so we could understand most of what he said, he replied, "the Captain will come soon". Then, loud and clear, we heard the soul-stirring bugle-call "taran-tara" played by a Legionnaire in the rarefied air, high in the Hoggar Massif. It announced the end of the mid-day siesta and the Captain returned to duty and daily life resumed.

A friendly Captain greeted us with hand-shakes. He was not offended by our not understanding much of his French, but he muttered something about, "a foolish expedition". Kindly, he said we may stay in the traveller's rest shelter without charge.

The typical desert shelter, very clean inside, had mud walls, open gap windows and an earth floor, partitioned by archways into four cubicles each with two folding beds and two chairs. I sat down on one of the folding beds to rest and true to form, it folded, plonk!, onto the ground. This time we had a good laugh about it, for it was hardly like other mishaps along the way which had not been so amusing.

The Captain of this mountainous region was of the firm, soldierly sort. Although our days here were on the go, the most tiresome was the mental part in persuading him to let us go the remaining five hundred miles to Agadez, the last oasis. This was his territory and although we had the permit, he would not let us go into the Dunes of Jadal. His objection was our trailer. However, he was reasonable and said he would allow us to proceed if our trailer was taken off. By this time we were wise in the ways of the authorities and officials, who from the very beginning had disapproved of our venture and we left the Captain at his desk. We went to the desert vehicle garage which, we thought, would be the only place to solve our problem. At first the *directeur* of the garage spoke Arabic, then he spoke French and our discussion continued with words spoken slowly, like an elementary class. "I look at it!", he said coming outside to see the motorcycle and sidecar with its trailer standing near a bus, into which merchandise, bags and baggage were being loaded for its run to Agadez. " Non!", he said, "we cannot tow it," we understood him to say, "it will fall to pieces!", meaning that it was not strong enough to be pulled behind the bus at speed over rough ground for a long distance. Blenk and I were inclined to agree we would lose the trailer and everything in it so we tried hard to convey the urgency of our request. The trailer was not very wide, so we asked "could it be lifted to lay wheels up on the roof of the bus and lashed securely with our rope ?". "Yes!" - for this idea, he agreed. We were allowed to ride the motorcycle and sidecar without the trailer and proceed with our expedition, but, we must wait each week until there is a bus that has room on the roof to carry it.

Waiting for a bus!

The next Société Algerienne des Transport Tropicaux vehicle that would probably have room for our belongings and transport everything out of the Sahara into the French West African colony of Niger, was scheduled to depart in two weeks time.

Desert vehicles were functional, but by no means beautiful. The driver's seat was raised high up to see over two radiators mounted on top of each other[1].

When ready to leave here for the journey to Agadez, the bus looked rough and ready with wares of all sorts stacked on the roof, hand luggage and water bags hanging around the exterior and passengers crammed inside with turbaned heads leaning out of bare window frames. With our trailer on board, we came away wondering if we would ever see it again!

During our short stay here, we walked to the camel market. There were pack camels, riding camels and a few runner camels for sportsmen who liked to race them. Camels have a prominent part in the lives of desert people and even today in the age of our super-trucks and helicopters or motorcycle, the camel is still the most satisfactory means of transport across sand.

When a camel caravan that may have been travelling twenty-five miles a day for ten days, without food or water, transporting their precious 350,000 lbs of commodities such as salt, grain, sugar and almost everything for human survival arrived at an oasis, there was considerable activity.

One mile south of the market place, camel tracks from the West (Timbuktu); the East (Bilma); the North (Ghardaia) and the South (Agadez) intersected in the desert sands making Tamanrhasset the cross-roads of the Sahara. A friendly Arab lowered two camels down to their knees for Blenk and me to mount and ride. The leather rein which the guide put in my left hand, went under the neck from a ring through its right nostril. He put my feet cross-ankled in the curve of its soft hairy neck, then made it ungracefully lurch, without me falling off, to get up its hind legs first. With each lilt or movement of its walking stride, my feet would goad or prod the neck as it went along. Somehow I could sense the camel knew I didn't know how to ride!

[1] *These are almost certainly the Laffly 4-ton 'Colonial' trucks specially built in 1933 for desert service. The additional radiator is quite small and sits, externally, on top of the radiator header tank. It is doubtless an engine oil cooler. BMJ.*

While we were in the Hoggar Massif we had peeked at a lifestyle that had been going on for centuries. In convoy, a rope from the camel's nose-ring is tied to the saddle of the one in front, so fastening forty or so camels together in a 'string'. Often as many as thirty strings, amounting to 1,200 beasts of burden came all together in single file, stretching out a very long way to make up a caravan. Two people ride in seats slung across its back, being about the same weight, give or take a few pounds, as a load carried in convoy. If a camel is not well trained, it can be very stubborn and nasty, kicking or biting and becoming quite dangerous with no liking for its master. An Arab or Tuareg, wrapped in a flowing garment, is sometimes not easily recognised, even by his own friends, but can be singled out by his camel and the way he rides. The saddle has a rounded seat with a high shaped pummel in the design of the Tuareg symbol, a 'Croix du Sud' - the constellation of the Southern Cross.

In the market place, booths were scattered around. At each stage of our journey the price of food and fuel became more expensive. Packaged food and processed nutrition were unheard of in those days, so we bought dates, jam, powdered milk and like natives, fed off the land. Bread was our staple food. Flour to make our bread had to be obtained from the quarter-master in charge of supplies and taken to the local baker. Blenk had no idea how much flour was needed for a loaf of bread and I did not know how much bread could be made from a kilo of flour! We had to convert our British shillings and ounces into French francs and kilos. On scraps of paper we estimated the amount of flour to buy to make enough bread for two of us for six days. The cheerful man selling it spoke Arabic and Hausa, but could not understand our figures because it was a bigger order than usual. He checked the figures and the quantity, but no one could agree about weight, quantity or price. At last calculations came close and we bought four kilograms of flour to take to the baker who said our bread would be ready on the day we were to leave. Meanwhile, we had other things to do.

The next morning two mounted Legionnaires leading two harnessed horses, each mounted with native trim and decorative trappings, courtesy of the Captain, came trotting along the palm-lined way to our shelter. They had come to take us for a ride beyond the oasis and to gallop over the sand. The Legionnaires, wearing typical *kepi* headdress, sat astride these 'drinkers of the wind', were silhouetted against the blue sky, resembling character heroes in a movie. The wind blew the tails of the horses sideways, just as it had lashed us up on the Tademait plateau, a few days ago. Riding horseback in the Sahara with the French Foreign Legion made amends for the hardships we had endured to reach here. It was another highlight of our expedition to be remembered.

The personnel stationed at outposts in the Sahara were extraordinary individuals. They were Legionnaires of regiments of the French Foreign Legion. The Legion is a voluntary army of a relatively small, closely united company of soldiers and is perhaps the most interesting military force in the world. A recruit of any nationality is not required to give his real name, or age. His enlistment is accepted with no questions asked. An applicant must join on French soil, be physically fit and make an oath first and foremost that he will be loyal to the Legion for a term of five years. The saga behind that pledge is of a Legion that offers to any man in the world - who is unfortunately an outcast, for whatever reason, whether military, political, social or economic sufferer, or even a criminal. The regiment provides the ultimate life for a broken soul or an adventurous and brave spirit. This unit had served in the austere territory of North Africa for many years to subdue Moslem uprisings in Algeria and tribal raids on camel caravans to keep trade routes open, safe-guarding wireless installations at each oasis and taking care of search and rescue missions such as our breakdown contract.

When the Germans occupied France during World War II, the French Foreign Legion lost their 'nationality' and many of them, in loyalty to themselves, went to England to form the Free French forces. In the course of the war the British 7th Armoured Division and the Free French Legionnaires became known as the Desert Rats through their adoption of the jerbil as their insignia. Those Legionnaires, who were previously stationed in the Sahara in a combat zone they already knew well, returned to fight the German General Rommel, known as the Desert Fox, contributing to the Allied victory. During the more recent Desert Storm conflict in the Middle East, the Legion was again in action in familiar desert warfare. The Legion of Foreigners, as they are sometimes called, has no great record of victories, but their tradition is one of severe discipline and great courage in campaigns all over the world, that it was a privilege for us to become acquainted with them as 'one and all' symbolised loyalty and integrity.

The Captain invited us to his residence for dinner one evening before leaving and once again we enjoyed a touch of civilised living. Officers in his regiment of the French Foreign Legion, whose duties were much the same as personnel at other outposts, were introduced in order of rank: Lieutenants, wireless operator, medic, cook and two new *fonctionnaires* who were quite mystified by the two *jeune femmes* travellers.

We were all seated around the long table arranged in lovely French style down the centre of the dining room. A well groomed Arab orderly on duty, in white uniform wearing scarlet sash, stood behind the Captain's chair waiting to serve the meal. In a soft voice the Captain lowered his head and Blenk and me, in respect, lowered our heads, but after a while of not being able to understand a word in French wondered what was being said for so long! We enjoyed a delightful, by comparison with our trek fare, *repas* of roast goat, fresh vegetables, canned peaches, delicious French pastries, red wine and good company.

To In Guezzam

Back at the desert garage, after a few days rest, we prepared our kit for the next part of the Sahara trek to Agadez, the last oasis. By the regrettable process of elimination, everything except life-support items had to remain here in the trailer. Without the extra capacity of the trailer, we put aboard ten litres of fuel in the tank and carried three 20-litre containers of fuel in the sidecar for the single-cylinder Panther engine and the cooking stove. Food and water was geometrically wedged into place taking into consideration weight distribution. Oil for the Panther, unobtainable for two thousand miles, included two quart cans of very thick SAE 70 viscosity engine oil.

The well at In Guezzam, in the southern Erg Chech, two hundred and fifty miles or about half way to Agadez, had a desolate wireless outpost, but there would be no fuel or food available. Then briefcase, log book, passports and other important papers, were pushed in. We had now to forfeit comfort and protection and the other contents in the trailer for a while and came away from the SATT garage wondering if we would ever see our things again. Everything was ready ... except the bread.

Bread was made daily. Bare loaves - no wrapping to keep it fresh and clean or preservatives to prevent it from getting hard and stale too soon. Late in the afternoon when we were due to depart, Blenk walked to the Bakery and returned shaking her head. "Non! Not ready yet, *demoiselle*", she said. Before sunset, I went to the baker and on the way I watched a metal-worker using age-old bellows to puff up a fire while shaping a Southern Cross. I very much wanted a souvenir to remind me of the Tuaregs and glorious desert nights under the constellation of the Southern Cross, but sadly I did not buy it as all non-essential items had to be omitted from our gear. I walked back to the shelter shaking my head at Blenk saying "... pas fini - not ready yet".

Early next morning, on the day of our departure, Blenk tramped over there again and soon came stomping back as she could not understand what had happened. "You!", she blamed me, "you got the decimal point in the wrong place". She went on, "there is ten times too much bread" and in the same breath, "all the shelves are filled - the whole place is full of bread!" She continued, "I asked which is ours. He turned with outstretched arms indicating all of it!". "Wal," she said, "he must have been baking all night with enough flour to feed a tribe. You've bought enough bread to last us to Cape Town!". All the bread was tightly packed in by splitting loaves into small pieces to fill in the gaps. The Captain stipulated a six day time allowance under the breakdown contract for us to reach the wireless outpost at In Guezzam.

At daybreak, on 18th January, 1935, on and off duty soldiers were at the rest shelter to bid us 'Adieu!'. I glanced back to wave good-bye and have a last look at the Saharan refuge as we rode away with ends of the long French bread sticking up here and there, smelling like a *boulangerie*.

Trailer-less

Steering into the blue, or I should say yellow, the bright dazzling glare from the vast expanse of yellow sand was so intense almost to lead to sun-blindness and further squinting through tinted wrap-around glasses diminished our field of vision so much, we could not always see clearly the ground ahead to avoid dangerous places. The sidecar wheel dropped into a hollow, but without the trailer to steady it, we tipped sideways with the Panther lying over sidecar.

Fortunately no harm was done - no water had spilled and only a few drops of fuel leaked from the tank's filler cap. We gathered up our scattered belongings and carried on as if nothing had happened.

Down the Hoggar Massif, descending 1,000 ft, skimming over sand dunes like surfing sea waves, we grappled drifts with high revs in low gear. It was like tackling hazards in a club trials event. Chiding each other several times about intentionally picking out every rock and rift and nearly having us both fall off; we kept rolling along. We fell about three feet over an unseen rim that put a strain on every nut and bolt. Blenk on the 'Moseley' rear mudguard pillion seat, came down just right to hold on to something, saving herself from being dumped. Dark patches of hard mineral ground were showing up through the sand here and there and between them were these treacherous hollows of powder like sand. We pounced from one hard patch to another to skim across these sand-traps until they became longer, deeper and softer and eventually they trapped our wheels. Everything was unloaded again, carried across and then the unladen combination coaxed through these dangerous sink holes, while we sung the oarsman's chant, "One - two - PUSH!".

The fuel we calculated using had not made allowance for actual engine running time when wheel-spinning, churning up the sand or zig-zagging to avoid very bad places. Besides, slow progress was taking up our breakdown contract allowance in temperatures ranging from 125°F in the daytime to a chilly below 50°F night. All the while the Panther and ourselves worked harder, but our average speed decreased. Central Sahara is one of the hottest places on earth in mid-summer. It seldom rains there and the hot ground would melt the soles off our shoes. Overland travel between these outposts would surely cease in time - hopefully, even at our snail-pace, we would not still be here by then![2]

In the rocky north, there were the *hammadas*, like the Tademait plateau; then the windswept *reg* area strewn with flint and sharp stones causing us numerous flat tyres. We crossed a *wadi*, a dried up river bed, which was an obstacle all of its own, then in the bottom of great basins were the ergs, those vast puddles of sand in which we were now in the middle. We followed the line of least resistance southward towards In-Guezzam between rocks and sand drifts along a twisty course like that of a *wadi* where once upon a time a river may have flowed in different directions towards its destiny.

Our log book lost count of which day it was, or whether we slept or rode some nights, so we were unable to tell how much time remained on the breakdown contract to reach In-Guezzam and the wireless outpost.

The constellation of the Southern Cross appeared overhead as daylight faded beside a myriad of other stars and we stopped to sleep, feeling that In-Guezzam was not far away. We had enough cocoa to add to the insipid water to make the night beverage and by now the bread was quite hard.

---

[2] *Indeed, a trans Saharan railway line had already been planned in the late 1930s from Morocco to Timbuktu, but came to nought. BMJ.*

Little fussing to sit down and be comfortable on a nearby rock, I accidentally tipped over my mug of cocoa and it spilled. The sand drank it.

Sighted

The sun came up anew the next morning. In a marvellous moment of surprise a light air plane appeared in the sky and swooped low overhead as if to dive in salute. Whether the plane was on a 'Lign du Hoggar' flight-path or a military reconnaissance mission we did not know, but its brief appearance boosted our spirits immensely, as we had not seen a living thing between the outposts where nothing lives, or can live - not even flies. A long time later, I found out that it was sent by a London weekly publication.

> "The French military plane swooped low to examine the speck crawling slowly on through the illimitable burning wastes of the Sahara. Unbelievable sight. Two girls on a motorcycle and their equipment. With their precious load of petrol and still more precious water, they were travelling steadily south, blazing a new trail to Nigeria. Hence through Equatorial Africa, taxing women and machine to the limit of endurance - to Nairobi and the all-red route to the Cape, Wonderful machine. Indomitable pair. Heroes of an achievement besides which every motorcycle record pales into insignificance."[3]
>
> *The Motor Cycle*

Tired and weary, yet having to be alert as we neared In-Guezzam, both of us were very much on the lookout for any trace of habitation or sign of life. The rider was the close-up spotter seeking to avoid or negotiate hazardous places, while the pillion passenger was the long-range observer. Heat haze made things visible, then vanish. Was it another mirage? Wind had blown sand heaped against the mud wall surrounding the tiny fort. Bare of palm trees, it was almost indiscernible in the distance, resembling a line of rocks along the ground and by not giving it enough attention, we nearly overlooked the place by-passing the fort entirely, which would have had disastrous consequences for us.

To prevent such a calamity from happening to any traveller, the Duty Sentry, standing on the mud roof, used a primitive method to signal us by using two mirrors (a heliograph) to converge brilliant beams of sunlight to flicker them on us and attract our attention. Suddenly it became a moment of joy. We had been contacted! Yes, there it was, In-Guezzam. We could now actually see the wireless masts and altered our course slightly westward and steered towards the fort.

---

[3] *This passage later appeared in an advertisement for Geo Clarke, who had prepared the motorcycle combination for the expedition. BMJ.*

We had crossed the Grand Erg Occidental, as this region was known, with little search-and-rescue time, fuel or water to spare.

At the gate in the mud wall surrounding the wireless outpost, the operator stood ready to meet us with a broad grin on his face and with a hearty handshake, he shouted, "Bravo ... BRAVO!". At that moment, as fate would have it, the rear tyre had yet another puncture.

With the camels in the desert

Agadez – The Last Oasis
In Guezzam To Agadez

Two French civilian helpers pushed the Panther, with its flat tyre, into the compound as we walked behind, feeling not the slightest remorse about letting them do it. If we had tyre trouble anywhere else, I don't know what would have happened, as we now found that the tyre pump was defective and the new tube couldn't be inflated. In Guezzam was a grateful half-way respite in the long distance of vast Saharan wasteland between Tamanrhasset and the last official wireless controlled outpost at the oasis of Agadez. Here was a refuge and relief for a short while after five days of the burden imposed on us by time, water and physical exertion. This tiny wireless outpost at In Guezzem, about half way to Agadez, enclosed an area of only a few hundred square yards and was staffed by just a few French civilians. The man in charge said our tyre pump would be repaired and took it to the workshop where he laid it on the bench, but feeling somewhat travel worn, we were in no hurry for it.

The well that gave name to this place was in the centre of the compound, opposite the gateway in the mud wall surrounding the place. The civilian in charge did not offer us accommodation in the traveller's quarters like the Legionnaires elsewhere had done, so that night it was just as easy for us to sleep on the outside of the mud wall, than to pay the price of bare accommodation on the inside. Anyhow, we were within reach of help. After dark, light glowing from a fire illuminated the unsymmetrical arches of the inner compound as we strolled across the compound with our sleeping bags and walked out into the desert, to sleep by the south wall for best protection from the wind. Fortunately the night was mild, as the linings of our sleeping bags had been left behind with the trailer at Tamanrhasset.

Tired from an almost complete crossing of the Sahara, we laid on the soft sand beneath the vast expanse of the Heavens. Listening to the silence, I felt the breeze fan my face. The constellation of the Southern Cross appeared angled, like a tilted sword and the two brightest stars were in line with the South Pole. In no other way could nights be so tranquil as those under desert sky. The peace was suddenly broken as a small lizard, seeking shelter, crawled inside my sleeping bag. I jumped up all of a sudden, shrieking and stamping around, shaking my sleeping bag all over the place to fling it away, frightening Blenk out of her wits. When the commotion was all over, the quiet night returned, allowing us to fall sound asleep.

At daybreak we rolled up our sleeping bags and walked through the gap in the mud wall back to the compound. Along the south wall, on the left of the gateway, were the dining room, kitchen, store rooms and staff living quarters. Along the north wall, on the right side, were the travellers' quarters laid on an earth floor and separated by open archways, each with two beds, two chairs, a small table and a couple of candles. Opposite the gateway, behind the well, were the wireless control room and workshops. We found our tyre pump was still laying on the bench - perhaps nobody knew what to do about it? It was time for us to move along, so to make a diaphragm for the plunger-rod, I cut off the leather tongue from one of my shoes, soaked it in engine oil and inserted it into the pump body to form a leather pump washer and proceeded to pump up the inner tube. It worked - the rear tyre inflated.

To Agadez

We spent another night by the south wall just outside the compound and crossed the open Algerian border into French West Africa the next morning. We had accumulated about five different kinds of currency, but had no coins of the realm to pay for anything here, but fortunately French Francs were accepted. We bought an expensive can of corned beef, refilled with water and filled the tank and a ten litre fuel can with petrol.

The worst part of the Sahara was supposed to be behind us. We had crossed the Hoggar Massif and were now not so worried about going astray, getting lost or suffering water shortages which had accounted for the fate of other unfortunate venturers. But the Southern Erg still stretched southward a long way beyond In-Guezzam.

The wireless operator gave an accurate description of conditions for the next three hundred or so miles, almost the longest hop. He explained that coming away from the Hoggar Massif and descending to a lower altitude, deep sand and huge dunes formed the Southern Erg. The ascent to another plateau, the Air Massif, en route to Agadez would be difficult, if not impossible for a motorcycle.

Water could be found at the Well of In-Abangarit, about one hundred and twenty-five miles due south - if we could find it - but the water, though sweet, would have to be boiled first. Another well was at Tegguidda n'Tessoum, sixty miles further south and at In-Gal, a Fulani settlement about seventy-five miles west of Agadez. To be completely free from the jurisdiction of SATT breakdown contracts on the southern edge of the desert, we were allowed six days, calculated on our life-support rations, to reach Agadez - the last oasis.

At daybreak on 20th January, 1935 we were ready to ride the last Saharan hop or *hadj*, as the Arabs say. The wireless operator sent out his regular transmission to Agadez and received one from Tamanrhasset, then went for his morning walk in the boulder-strewn direction. Soon after leaving, I turned to look back and have a last glance of the mud wall surrounding In Guezzam; it looked like a wooden pole laying on the ground, just as it had at first sight.

The day's run was spasmodic - a good run, then getting stuck; another good run, then stuck again, just as we had done so many times before, prospecting around with our heels for hard ground. Unladen, the motorcycle dashed across deep powder-like places. We carried our things across to ground hard enough for us to move again and slowly we got along. We must have passed both the wells at In-Abangarit and Tegguidda, or we were slightly off course.

As it was getting dark, Blenk again prepared camp and I prepared the evening snack. "Tea is ready", I said. But, provoked by Blenk heading to the tool-box as if to do something to the Panther, I repeated, "TEA is READY". "Yes," she said, "I'm getting the screwdriver to split the bread!" Joking aside, we counted the number of times and different ways to break, split or soak the huge, miscalculated, amount of bread which still proved to be edible after so much had been made in Tamanrhasset, more than a week ago. So with hard bread and jam, we ended another day.

No notes had been written in the log book, though none were needed anyway to remind me of this part of the journey, but neither could we tell which day it was, or how much time remained on the breakdown contract. The sun sent down maximum heat from a clear blue sky. Relief from exertion of rushing, pulling and lifting whenever we got stuck, was just a mouth-rinse of brackish and quite hot water. A mirage appeared of graceful palm trees and a flowing stream of water, but again we knew better than to be tricked by these optical illusions.

Nearing the southern fringe of the Desert the landscape changed. Hard bumpy ground clearly showed a track and parched scrub land vegetation, striving for growth in this Sahel Region. It was a transitional stage between desert and 'Black Africa'. We were pleased now to travel in a higher gear and a little faster. Unfortunately there was also a change in the sound of the motor and a drop in power, Blenk said to herself, "this thing doesn't sound right." I asked her, "... something clattering?". The intense heat had thinned the viscosity of the lubricating oil and the engine stopped. The con-rod bearing had broken through lack of effective lubrication.

Breakdown

In every situation so far, we had been able to worm our way out of trouble, but were quite at a loss to know what to do in this sad situation. All other breakdowns, one way or another, had been taken care of, but without a workshop to dismantle the engine and fit new parts, no fire of ingenuity could handle this problem. The fact we were stranded here was terrifying. Our location could only be estimated. Agadez outpost was quite another hundred miles away. Overdue, our search-and-rescue contract, at four francs a kilometre each way, would cost us a lot of money. If only the engine would start, just once more....

We hoped that by using constant revs to keep the main bearing 'floating', there was a ghost of a chance we could coax a few more miles. Fuel was of no use to us any more. Water was more precious. We dare not fail. There is no help like self-help, so we had to push. Perhaps we could reach a settlement where there was water and save us a few hundred francs of rescue money?

We pushed it in the cool of night. Through the heat of day we pushed on and on past withered tufts of shrubbery between what looked like enormous heaps of sand, but were in fact ant-hills. Pushing from the rear was easier than from the side and we swapped our positions from steering to pushing many times. We tied the handlebars with rope to go straight ahead so we could both push from behind, but the laden sidecar veered to one side and the rope slackened and got tangled. This well intended idea proved unsatisfactory, wasting much time and effort. We continued to push to the rhythm of popular tunes swapping our positions once again from pushing or steering while singing and kicking up the dust.

"Is this a motorcycle expedition or a walking trip?", I heard Blenk comment, but I kept quiet and went on pushing. We came to a huge mound of stones built like a beacon with a stick at the top, then in the distance a smaller heap but no stick; presumably to mark a half-kilometre indicating clearly the direction to follow. So, we were definitely on the right track. We argued about how many more sticks there were as we pushed our way along and how many francs per kilometre we saved of our search party fee. I believe this is what kept us going.

After a while we stopped to boil water for tea and a snack of very hard bread and jam. We laid on the ground for a short sleep until daylight. Meanwhile nomads from a nearby well settlement near In-Gal had seen our dust rising and since any sign of movement in the desert was a call-to-arms, told their Chief. In the early morning, he sent out his scouts to look around. At the light of dawn, we woke to see a cavalry of mounted tribesmen galloping in this direction. They came upon us with a halt so abrupt, that the wild-eyed horses reared on their hind legs, pawing the air as we stood up gazing helplessly; too fatigued to be afraid. Panting Arabian horses with flared nostrils circled us as we faced four Fulani tribesmen for what seemed hours, but was in fact only minutes, as they gave stirring shouts in their native tongue. The leader dismounted within arms length of us and held out a goat skin water bag. Using our rope, one of the horses towed us to their settlement about five miles away. We had reached In-Gal. If we had not pushed so far they would not have seen our dust rising.

The Chief of the Fulani tribe and his headman, an elderly herdsman with wrinkled face and smiling friendliness, received us on the southern edge of the Sahara with quaint courtesy. They paid their respects by sending along a young woman with two small bowls of *couscous*, a local pasta prepared by grinding raw wheat, hand rubbing the flour into tiny grains and then cooking it over steam and serving it in goats milk. Sheep and goats were taken out of a shelter to make room for us for the night. A make-shift bed they carried in had two legs to support the head end and a wooden box to support the foot end while the mattress looked and smelt as if goats had laid on it - which they probably had! However nothing that night disturbed our sound sleep.

In the morning a tribesman who learned to speak English at a Mission school, was called in. This fine young man came along and made it clear to us everything that the Chief had said. The Chief wanted to know the reason for us being here in French West African. All the while, our breakdown contract allowance was ticking away. Tribal folk gathered around, squatting and watching us like children at a puppet show. Fulani people living in stretched goat-skin tents, filled their water bags at the well and made fire from heat-friction by a pointed stick of hard wood pressed into soft wood and spinning it by hand, in much the same way as their forefathers of Old Testament days. Then the Chief wanted to know if we ate meat? We were dreaming of perhaps a sandwich, a stew or other concoction quite unaware that it was not their custom to slaughter an animal for food except on a special occasion. Fulani natives butchered the carcass and hung portions on tent-poles and wherever else the meat could be suspended. Flies immediately covered it all, so until barbecued, rather than hickory or oak smoked, it was 'fly-cured'.

In the remaining three days of our breakdown time limit to reach Agadez, the Chief agreed to loan us two horses and tow us the seventy-five miles to Agadez. His son and the Mission youth were to go with us as guides and return with the horses. Our money was not valid here, but most likely the Captain of that region would be able to exchange currency to pay two hundred local francs for the men and the horses. The journey there and back would take the young men about a week. We were lucky they had horses and considering the arduous nature of the safari, the amount seemed very reasonable - but then we had no choice as the SATT search party expense would be much more. In our woeful situation the Mission boy was such a great help translating English to the Hauna tongue spoken by these indigenous people. As he made such clear communication with the Fulani Chief, we gave him the fresh sheepskin.

A one horse-power Panther

The trek to Agadez left on 25th January. The Chief's son, robed in a flowing indigo cloth like a Tuareg, mounted his four-legged horse to tow our iron horse, on which I sat steering, while Blenk sat astride the relief horse intending to change saddles with me every so often. The pace set to cover the distance in time was too fast for the nimble-footed Mission youth that the relief horse soon had two people on its back. Our escort were magnificent lads who knew a great deal about the Sahel Region. They stopped at midday at a place, shored up with sticks and circled with stones, not marked on our chart, which irrigated a patch of vegetation concealed by boulders. We were able to rest and water the horses. Even if we were dying of thirst, we would never have found this place. They lowered a billy can on the end of the rope, ten feet down a dark hole, to bring up water. They lighted a fire, as water always had to be boiled, made tea and reheated the leftover mutton. It was quite some time before it was finished. We chewed at it, holding a chunk of mutton with both hands as befitted the occasion. Things were bundled away and the pilgrimage literally dragged on. It was my turn on horseback.

That night, the Chief's son was hardly able to stay awake and he nodded off in the saddle, letting his horse pull us around scrub and clusters of bushes, zig-zagging its way along, quite oblivious of where he was going. On several occasions he only awoke as he was about to fall off his horse. Then it was my turn to steer the Panther again and I tried to take the strain off the steering over the soft sand by putting my feet hard against the handlebars. The tow rope broke! Where there was good footing, climbing a thousand feet up the Air Massif increased the pace to only three miles an hour. Again the tow rope broke and re-knotted each time, it got shorter. Now we were much too close to the back of the horse!

The most dreary time was the hour before dawn. We all laid on the ground for a nap until awakened by the sun ... and the flies. These young men had by now done the hardest days' work of their lives. The mission boy told us that all the way along, the Chief's son tried to convert him to the Moslem religion. About thirty more miles to Agadez and another dose of daytime heat. We had only eleven hours of daylight left before the search-and-rescue contract would be put into effect. Switching horses did not make them go any faster; they wearily stumbled along doing their best.

About twelve more miles to tow and three hours before sunset, we forgot the heat and the discomforts. Along the way, our shadows measured their length on the sand. Even the horses seemed to know this odyssey was ending. Desert sunset had faded to dusk when one of the boys pointed languidly ahead to the tall obelisk of the Mosque of Agadez, etched like a symbol of triumph on the evening sky. The eighteen hundred miles of Saharan drama now lay behind us.

Agadez

It had taken us a month to accomplish the crossing and we reached the last oasis with only a few minutes of our breakdown contract to spare. Captain Bernard de Romefort, of the Agadez region, came away from an evening game of tennis to confirm our arrival as we signed in and were taken to the traveller's rest shelter.

Some time later, a startling fact was revealed to us. The SATT vehicle from Tamanrhasset had been delayed and the mail truck on its run to Zinder, had not yet returned. As it happened, there was no suitable desert vehicle immediately available for rescue duties. The thought crossed my mind that had we not made the effort to get ourselves out of trouble when the engine failed by pushing the motorcycle such a long way, but had waited back there for help to come and considering our shortage of food, water, fatigue and the heat, what would have happened to us? We might very likely have met the same fate as that camel whose bleached bones we saw lying along the wayside.

Stranded!
Agadez

In the early morning sunshine, standing under the entrance archway of the bare mud hut, on the southern edge of the Sahara, we looked around from where we had been taken for shelter in the darkness of the night before. Straight ahead, about ten minutes walk away, the French *Tricolore* fluttered over Fort Militaire, blown by a dry wind. I stood there awhile thinking about our difficulties over the rough terrain, administrative encounters, mechanical problems and the physical hardships we had overcome to reach here, and how I could hoist a moral banner for the feeling of inner joy and excitement of a *fait accompli* - my mind fluttered like that flag.

Now, in daylight, I turned to see the Mosque of Agadez as a symbol of our accomplishment. Unlike other places where the well and fort were completely surrounded by a mud walls, the wireless outpost, military barracks, rest shelter, market and neighbourhood homes at Agadez, were all spread over a wide area. So far, this was only the first part of traversing the entire African continent on our ride to Cape Town. Stranded on the oasis with an unusable motorcycle for the foreseeable future, we contemplated how to continue the journey. After struggling against time, we now had time on our hands!

With fresh clothes and clean faces, we walked off to see the Captain of the Air Massif region. As the commander here, he was very kind and helpful. He told us there would be no charge to stay in the traveller's rest shelter however long we had to wait to repair our motorcycle. The Captain sorted our accumulated, but invalid currency. He told us the Chief at In-Gal would be paid and he exchanged it for local francs. We paid the two excellent guides who had helped with their horses and also for the slaughtered sheep.

Speaking French very slowly, the Captain explained, "a wireless message for new parts will be sent to P&M (Phelon & Moore's) factory in Yorkshire, England, and procedures will soon be under way to obtain them." Then he told us, "new engine parts would be flown to Algiers, then brought across the desert by the SATT trans-Saharan vehicle," but, he continued, "it would depend on how much the bus could carry with baggage and merchandise already loaded - and if there is no room for your shipment, you must wait another week for the next vehicle", and so on. Nothing could be done until the day our new parts arrived. We could only hope - and wait.

Meanwhile, the days spent in these harsh, though interesting, surroundings were priceless. Our nights were quiet and peaceful and we lost little sleep worrying about our predicament, as difficult situations on an arduous expedition like this were apt to occur. The Captain in Tamanrhassett was right about us not being able to get across the Dunes of Jadal, in the Southern Erg, towing a trailer, for we would have been hopelessly stuck in deep hollows and discarding items along the way to save weight, we would have lost everything. Until new parts arrived from home in due course, we could not overhaul the Panther engine. Until the trailer with all our belongings was reattached to the motorcycle, we were stranded.

Soon, Legionnaires of the French Foreign Legion walked from their barracks carrying two folding beds for us to lay on. Before long they came again with two chairs - and again, with a small table and candles, then again with a large mat to cover the earth floor. Almost every day they returned with something or other for our comfort, including a crate on which to stand the wash bowl and water pitcher, not forgetting some dishes and clean linen. Someone with a sense of humour hung a cheerful picture on the mud wall so that this stark empty place we had stumbled into a week ago, was by now short of space. Then, along came a gramophone to cheer our gloomy spirits with music. We played over and over again the only disc which was not chipped or cracked and whenever I hear that tango and the popular tune on the other side, they always remind me of Adagez and the French Foreign Legion.

At the far right end of the shelter, four wooden posts were rammed into the ground to make an enclosed space, about four feet square, wrapped around with burlap material for a bathroom. A fuel container perforated with nail holes, and filled with water carried in by a native from the nearby well for the price of a small tip, was hung from a hook overhead. It sprinkled water long enough to have a good shower while standing on a board over a drainage ditch.

Tauregs of the Kel Air tribe, living in goat or camel skin tents were scattered around us. A big tent was formed from as many as a hundred goat skins sewn together. The back of the tent sloped inward. As nomads, they moved along now and then to a fresh place, taking with them the tent and a low fenced enclosure for their livestock, but kept close to the oasis. Apart from their tribal tongue, Arabic was their only language and the Koran, their spiritual communication. Children were taught by their families to write in the sand.

Desert life awakened as the sun went down. Tuareg families came from outside with mats to see the spectacle of sunset and the night sky brighten with stars to glorify the heaven.

A Hausa settlement, not far away, had fixed dwellings where posts in the ground supported communal hut walls with flat roofs, standing side-by-side in very narrow streets, like passageways. In parts of the world where the sun is hot and there is a shortage of wood, sun-dried mud-brick material makes good insulation against heat or cold and dates back thousands of years. At first glance their earth coloured dwellings were not easy to discern.

The Hausa are a negro people; their market attracted one and all. When the market closed at dusk, their remaining wares and livestock were taken back to their camp. Roaming around the native market here was no more fraught with danger than the streets in my home town.

One evening after dark, with nothing to do, we strolled into the Hausa settlement in prankish mood, taking a bed sheet with us. In those days we had no radio to listen to or television to watch, nor the ability to read foreign language newspapers. Along a narrow street, not much wider than a western pavement, between two rows of dwellings, we waited in a doorway until a man on a donkey carrying a pack from market passed by and another poor beast, coaxed along by a rider swinging his skinny legs and feet which almost scraped the ground. The faster the swinging, the faster the donkey tried to get along. Then Blenk scrambled up to sit on my shoulders. She draped the white sheet over her head, wrapping it around us down to my feet, to look tall, thin and ghostly. In this garb we stepped slowly past a few stray goats to scare some natives. Some souls knelt in prayer to guard against the super-natural, children vanished from sight and those who guessed right lingered and did nothing. The joke was good for a laugh, but as we heard afterwards, our idea of entertainment may not have turned out to be so funny.

Sometimes we walked to the small smoke filled cafe, lit by lanterns, near the Mosque where we mingled with the crowd. Her Royal Highness, the Duchess d'Oasta, sister of the King of Italy, had come to Agadez to evade the European winter, arriving by camel caravan with light wicker furniture for her comfort. Her servants bought extra supplies and camped in tents. In the cafe, we were introduced to the Duchess who cordially greeted us. Speaking perfect English, she invited us to visit her in camp. One evening we walked a few minutes beyond the well to where Her Royal Highness had pitched her tents. We dined with our royal hostess in exquisite style and in her presence, ladylike for a while, we used her knives and forks rather than our fingers.

A desert trip

A month went by still waiting for parts to come from the factory to repair the Panther, when someone suggested a jaunt in the mail truck to the south-west corner of French Equatoria to see a bit more of the country. At 1.00 am in the morning, on a cool night of 21st February, the loaded mail truck was ready to depart for Dosso, a distance of about four hundred miles each way. Two competent official mailmen in a huge but trustworthy truck, like an armoured battleship, went dashing away over monotonously flat barren ground at sixty miles an hour behind the powerful headlight beams. What a ride!

At dawn, ostrich were seen and in disturbing their peace and quiet, they stood up and ran away. One of the crew levelled a rifle through the open truck window and took aim, but ostrich are fleet-of-foot and can stride at about forty miles an hour. We gave chase dodging about, but the lovely birds out manoeuvred us and I was glad they got away, if only to save the truck from becoming a wreck.

The largest of living birds, though unable to fly, they have keen eyesight and will rest with their long neck stretched out over the ground on the lookout for danger with only a heap of feathers to be seen, giving the impression that ostriches hide their heads in the sand. Driving for hours over earthy ground, in this sparsely populated French colony, the driver avoided sparse bushes and parched trees striving for growth. At last, at a short stretch of road approaching Dosso, we were left to probe around a travellers rest shelter by a village of thatched round huts by ourselves. These were of one of perhaps seven probable tribes. The truck went on to Dosso and the mailmen went about their business of collecting and delivering mail. They arranged to pick us up a day later on their return journey. Here, in an open air market, I had my first taste of mango fruit.

The shipment of new parts had not yet arrived by the time we returned to Agadez, nor was there any sign of our trailer and belongings from Tamanrhasset. There was not much time left, for soon the SATT vehicles, camel caravans and wireless outposts would stop operating in the hot season.

One afternoon siesta time, I left my shoes by the gateway to our rest shelter. Later when I came to wear them again, I could not believe my eyes. The sun had come around, burning down on them for an hour or so and having shrivelled them so much, I could no longer wear them! The other pair was miles away in the trailer. The ground was much too hot to stand without shoes, so Blenk walked to market to find me something to wear. Footwear made by the natives to tread over sand had wide soles and she carried back a pair holding one sandal in each hand saying, "this is all I can find" and laughed at me when I trod on the wide part with the other foot and flopped over.

Another time, with nothing much else to do, she checked the first aid kit for any eventuality that might occur in the tropics and discovered the needle in the snake-bite pack did not fit the syringe. She said we should see the medic about it and he willingly exchanged it.

The Captain planned a barbecue party one weekend at his residence to which Blenk and I were invited. That evening, arriving through full-length glass pane double doors, we joined the social gathering where a long table with white cloth was laid in delightful French style. It was spread with chef-cooked food and local fruit. As the sun went down, a bonfire burned on the patio outside. Two orderlies, bearing a goat carcass slung by the feet from a rod or spit, carried it shoulder-to-shoulder in the very same way the early French settlers used to roast the native goat, beard-to-tail, or as the French say *barb-en-queue* (from which comes barbecue). The goat was held low over the hot embers, turning the grill slowly over and over, stepping around the fire while the party was going on in the dining room. The Captain was given the word when the meat was cooked. Everyone arose from the table, holding knife in hand and went outside to the patio from where the smell of roast meat and a touch of seasoning was coming, to carve off for themselves luscious chunks of meat. We held them with the fingers and ate in the traditional *barb-en-queue* style. Apart from the good food, more than anything else, the occasion was an opportunity to experience the traditional customs in the jovial company of Officers and men of the French Foreign Legion.

A field workshop

At last news came over the wireless that the SATT transport had left Tamanrhasset. Late one afternoon, at the end of February, I saw it come rumbling along in the distance, pass behind bushes before it was in full view again. High up there on the roof was our dear old maroon trailer, even though it wagged like a stubborn donkey pulling at the halter. We could hardly wait for it for it to be unloaded. The trailer was just as we left it. It had no lock, so the contents were not secured, yet nothing was damaged or missing. Customs had cleared and released the new engine parts.

Phelon & Moore had been prompt in sending the parts. A new connecting-rod, complete with small-end bush, main bearing and all necessary seals and gaskets came packed inside a carton that once contained a bottle of whisky. The factory instructions for assembly read as follows:

> "The operation of completely dismantling the Panther engine should be done in the nearest Sheik's tent - preferably one with a good carpet on the floor, as this saves the mechanic's knees and also prevents ants from crawling in and making a mess of the oil filter.
>
> Flywheels should be replaced (unless lost) and should run at least to within a half inch of circular truth."

Another note on the carton said. "Sorry, we didn't have room to include the original contents."!

In the base workshop, with the help of a French mechanic whose metric tools did not fit our Whitworth gauge nuts and bolts, the Panther engine was carefully rebuilt and ran well as soon as it was kick-started. We were ready to continue the journey to Cape Town. Early in the morning of 4th March, 1935, Legionnaires came to the Rest Shelter to bid us "Adieu!" and Captain Favro presented each of us with a silver Tuareg Cross.

Riding in the desert

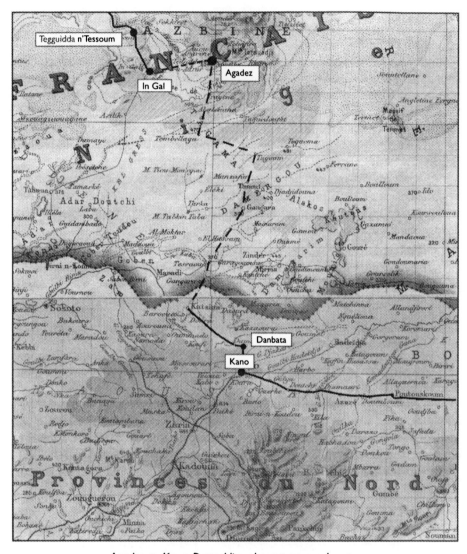

Agadez to Kano. Dotted line shows presumed route.

South Of The Sahara
Agadez To Kano

At just about the hottest time of the year, the rebuilt Panther engine had to be carefully handled to allow it to run in and prevent over-heating from pulling our heavy supplies. However over the next three days we would have to make up for time lost in Agadez. Within twenty miles from Agadez, the rear tyre was flat again; it was last repaired six weeks ago and 360 miles away back in In-Guezzam. This time however the inflator worked. Tools, too hot to handle, had to be kept under cover while we repaired the tyre and soon we were back on the track. The southern fringe of the Sahara, although still in French Equatoria was outside the range of SATT rescue as water could now be found. Even so it was just as difficult getting along, and the day's ride was almost the least distance we recorded. The Frenchman we met in Ghardaia, two thousand miles away, evidently knew what he was talking about when he told us Sahara conditions never ended until Kano. Apart from occasional gazelle or camel caravans, there was not a sign of life.

Riding alongside the track on virgin ground, between scrubby growth, sometimes offered better wheel grip, but we did not expect wildlife to be lurking there in these undisturbed places. Suddenly a snake, the first reptile we had seen out of captivity, slithered out and we reasoned thereafter to keep both eyes open for any creature, from harmful insects to big game, for we were approaching the Kingdom of African Wildlife. The track ran through windswept sand and scrub country over a succession of hard patches, where in places the going was easier and was marked by man-made heaps of stones about eighteen inches high - they were not always easy to see from a distance if they had toppled down or were hidden by scrub. Camel caravans taking different routes crossed here and there, obliterating track marks and making it difficult to pick out the correct path so as we did not get lost.

The motorcycle was bouncing around just as it had done without the trailer after the Captain in Tamanrhasset made us take it off. Blenk in an uproar from the sidecar, yelled, "Wal - turn round!" I turned in the saddle to look back. "What for ?", I wanted to know. "Well - " she over-stressed, "look again!". Again I looked behind saying, "I can't see anything". "Well that's why," she replied, " STOP - we've lost the trailer!".

I turned the motorcycle around and we went back to where the trailer had unhitched itself over the bumps, assuring her that I would have found out before we reached Cape Town, but my humour drew no comment.

Native villages, where negro Africans lived, were far apart on this semi-arid ground which was gradually being encroached upon by waves of drifting sand from the Sahara. The sands were eroding their productive land and were expanding hundreds of square miles a year which explains to a certain extent the plight of people in this part of Equatorial Africa. Like the nomads of the desert who do not have much, these people had to be constantly on the move in search of better land for crops and livestock, but when we came to a village close to the track they sometimes had produce to sell and we could refill our water cans. The sound of our motorcycle made natives at a village come running out and help push when we were stuck in the sand. Anywhere there was space for another black hand on our motorcycle, a native helped to push us along until, one by one, they went by the wayside and returned to their haunt. A good measure of thanks went to Tessoua and Hausa villagers for their willing and vigorous help along the sandy trail to Kano.

In the Tropic of Cancer a thatched roof on poles every ten miles or so provided shelter for travellers from the mid-day sun and we found out from experience during late morning and early afternoon, that riding on scorching hot ground was not practicable when, no where near shelter, the rear tyre went flat again. As we were lying on the ground alongside the track, in the shadow of the trailer while the sun passed overhead, a well equipped truck for rugged colonial conditions, came rumbling north, carrying administrative personnel on their way to Agadez. Surprised to see us there, it stopped. Blenk crawled from underneath the trailer and explained we were taking shelter while repairing a flat tyre and that the route to Kano was worse than expected.

In a village where we hoped to buy local food, natives were themselves strained as their land was being worn away by an encroaching fringe of the desert. To those people, money was of little benefit. The Code of the Wild (good fellowship) was such that these villagers insisted on giving us, without payment, two cans of beans and sausage, which from strangers in the wilderness, was like a gift from Heaven. But we were disheartened to be told the track was very bad for about another hundred miles. A Rest Shelter of round thatched-roof huts at Katsina village was a good place to stop for a snack and short rest for the remainder of daylight, then a night ride in brilliant moonlight. Conversation with any one of about two-hundred-and-fifty dialects spoken by ethnic groups here was reduced to sign language. To hold an empty can up-side down meant 'water' and to sound like a chicken clucking, meant 'eggs' or 'food'.

During the night ride before dawn, which seemed like about three o'clock in the morning (our wrist-watches had long since died), we laid on our coats spread on the ground under a tree for a nap. Awakened by sunrise, we were completely covered all over with a thick blanket of leaves, and if this day really was March 11th, then we had been exactly three months on this venture.

Nigeria

At the unmarked border, somewhere between French Equatorial colony of Niger and British Nigeria on the way to Kano, the rule of the road changed from 'keep to the right' to 'keep to the left'. Today the only vehicle we saw was now coming towards us and no matter which side Blenk steered, the driver of the on-coming car seemed intent on a collision course! In remote places, travellers always stop and greet each other and we both came to a standstill. The colonial settler speaking in basic English, was quick to voice reproof about us being on his wrong side. Blenk replied in good 'ole Cockney twang, "Sir - you may have crossed the border!". Perhaps we were now in Nigeria?

One after another we came to steep hillocks of some weird geological phenomenon like a roller-coaster in an amusement park, but less amusing with its steep humps, some on a curve and others straight ahead. We approached at full tilt by slick gear-changing to get up speed and rush to the top of one and come down with enough impetus to dash to the top of the next. Blenk hopped out of the sidecar to help push to the top of a hump and I heard her moaning in frustration, "This thing won't pull skin off a rice pudding", but she was not quick enough to leap on board again and unbeknown to me, I went on a distance without her.

On a track which was too narrow with the trailer to turn around, I waited for her topee to come bobbing up and down over the tall brown sun dried grass and yelled, "Blenk - where are you?" and then reassured her, "I would have noticed before arriving at Cape Town you were not here", but she still didn't say anything.

The square fibre block on the timing gear to drive the generator had worn smooth and the engine was no longer charging the battery. At turns as we twisted one way and another, hemmed in by grass five feet tall and with only the pilot light to see ahead, night riding became laborious until moonlight made it easier to trek along. Driving during the daytime on very hot ground was not a practical alternative to us loosing our lights.

In small villages leading to the metropolis of Kano, Nigerians wearing long white smocks in this awakening colony, were operating their own commercial trading posts. We stopped at one of these clusters of merchants to fathom out our loss of engine power and discovered it to be a broken valve-spring.

A loss of power

A corpulent merchant came down a rickety wooden stairway leading down the outside of his dilapidated little house and lead us back upstairs to his two rooms. With all three of us up there, the place seemed likely to cave in at any minute! He offered us tea and light refreshment and said this courtesy was given to white travellers. He told us that a "better and bigger place to break down" was four miles further along at Danbatta, only thirty miles from Kano. He told five Hausa youths to go with us and help push us over the steep hillocks. Slowly in low gear, one lad helped by pushing while the other walked easy, but at each steep incline on the rough see-saw road, all hands pushed to the top of each hillock until the road came alongside an irrigation canal. Tempted to jump in for a swim, they disappeared, leaving the last stretch of road to us to get along by ourselves.

Danbatta was a dirty place and prone to malaria, though we were well supplied with quinine tablets, a drug extracted from the bark of cinchona trees which we took as the mosquitoes emerged at sundown. We were allowed shelter in a grain storage shed. Inside was sour-smelling, alive with harmless little lizards scuttling about on the corrugated hutch catching flies - they had plenty to live on. We chose instead to camp out in the open, in full view of night walkers, not far from the trading post. Inside our tent, to which the mosquito net was fastened, it was much too hot so with the tent up, we tied all four corners of the net at the top to form a cone, diminishing the already small space inside. Eating was difficult; one hand held the plate, the other brandished the flies - more hands were needed!

Kano

An English rector and family at a Mission post in Kano, being better informed and more knowledgeable about local happenings than a press reporter, heard about our plight in suburban Danbatta and before we had time to fret about our trouble, came to find us and kindly towed us into town with their car. At the rector's bungalow, on the outskirts of the city, greetings lay in wait for Blenk and me with a cordial welcome by fellow country folk, hot water and a good meal. He offered to take us to the Colonial Office, the post office, go shopping and made arrangements to repair the motorcycle.

The 'Union Jack' flew above the Consul General's office, drooped about the mast in the calm air. It was the logical place to take our problem, "Yes -", said the Ambassador, and he went on to give consent for our motorcycle repairs to be done in the official workshop where government vehicles were maintained and overhauled by skilled mechanics. There was no need for us to do the work ourselves in the heat of mid-March - it was getting hotter every day. Cheerfully he said the engine would be put in good condition for us to continue our journey to Cape Town.

The Ambassador and staff were especially interested in our venture and our successful trans-Saharan crossing, for it brought this British colony many miles closer to the motherland. Car engine valve springs of comparable resilience and suitability to replace our broken and weak ones, were in stock thereby saving another long delay waiting for them to come from England, so with new inlet and exhaust valve springs and valves lapped in, the Panther engine would soon be restored to full power. Our misfortunes were usually like a rubber ball, since the harder we were put down by mishap, the higher we were to rebound - this time with a repaired engine!

Quarantined

An epidemic of Yellow Fever had not yet abated, so if we had not been detained by this engine problem, we would in any case have been quarantined.

For a thousand years, little was known about Nigeria. Kano, in its desert setting, was one of the ancient towns of Africa and the Hausa Kingdom. The old town of Kano was the largest exclusively Hausa city at the turn of twentieth century and the British built a new town around it with colonial homes and buildings constructed all over the place. Outside the Hausa district there was no regular plan and folk had to fend for themselves. The Moslem population lived exclusively within the twelve square mile metropolis of the old town of Kano, surrounded by a great mud wall at the end of the camel caravan routes. Donkey and camel-trains from adjoining districts and from across the Sahara, wormed their way through any of thirteen cowhide covered gates in a wall forty feet thick, as too did the disciples of Mohammed on their way to the Mosque and the market place. Whereas the old town of Kano were mainly Hausa peoples, white Nigerians, Europeans and other native tribes, lived and worked in the environs.

In the residential district away from native Kano, there were two rest shelters for white-race people, one being English and the other French. All the other transient accommodation was in the native district. The English rest shelter was the better one - elite, expensive with meals and maid-servants. The French shelter only had beds. It was not highly priced and was self-service. We went to stay there to fend for ourselves for an uncertain duration.

Kano was well-known for tanning hides and skins so that when the wind blew in the direction of our rest shelter, the smell of leather cured in arsenic drifted over. "People get used to it", said Blenk "so will we!". It was not long before her turn came at being affected by the nauseating stink. Once the wind changed and cleared the air, we both felt better.

Bicycles were everywhere. Some still had factory wrappers intact to protect chrome and paint work from losing their new gloss. Then, when the bicycle was well worn by hard use in sun and sand, the wrappers were taken off giving it a new-look appearance and then sold by the owner at a higher price!

While our motorcycle was being repaired in the workshops, we met interesting people including a Syrian gentleman who owned horses and took every possible precaution to protect his beautiful Arabian ponies from tsetse fly. These insects carried sleeping-sickness and were different from the mosquitoes which carried malaria or yellow fever. The tsetse fly has been and still is, a hindrance in the economic progress of Nigeria causing much loss of human life and livestock, as does it also in other parts of Africa. The horses needed daily exercise and nothing pleased the Syrian gentleman more than to let us ride them at any time we wished. Mounted on horseback, reined up like a pair of American cowboys, we went riding around shopping for food and things to get us ready to continue towards the equator.

We bargained like natives about things being worth the price asked, wondering how to evaluate something essential such as a hatchet for firewood and box of matches for the stove and camp fires. These fires warded off the wild creatures of the night, which were kept at bay by light.

We met a lady who said we should not leave Kano without tasting the Nigerian national dish of ground-nut (peanut) stew and invited Blenk and me to her home. Six of us sat at a round table enjoying a dish of home cooked Nigerian fare, listening to family tales of early colonial days and about the old folk at home, until time came to walk back to our shelter for the night. When we returned, I folded back my bed sheet and a thing with claw-like feelers and it's tail cocked up scampered out. I was told later it was a scorpion! It may not have been the only one in there and I should have remade my bed.

A Moslem ceremony

Today was Shawwal Day. Within the walled city a ceremony concluding *Ramadan*, the Holy ninth month of the Moslem year, was attended only by Moslems, but Tuareg, Hausa and Arabs who did not conform to the faith, came to Kano to observe the ritual. Blenk and I were invited to watch the sacred rite from the rooftop of a mud building, sitting on chairs overlooking the arena. Hundreds of Moslem worshippers, all wearing *gondoura* gowns, *tagelmoust* head dress and *takatkat* trousers, drawn in at the ankles, awaited the arrival of the Sultan of Kano. The Sultan came walking into view wearing the usual long white shirt-like garment and the desert *tagelmoust* veil, under cover of a bright coloured orange-and-yellow parasol which was being twirled round and round over him by an attendant. Dignitaries followed him to a position mid-field and then turned to face all those who had come to worship. The Sultan's armed bodyguards, mounted on magnificent white camels, each holding his sword with Southern Cross hilt, took positions equally left and right on either side of the Sultan. Tribal representatives and other dignitaries had also come on their lovely camels and lined up near the bodyguards, also turning to face the hundreds of Moslems who had come to worship. One by one, officers of the Sultan came forward and dismounted for prayer - quite an effort for each camel to get down on it's knees and raise up again on its long legs, but these were remarkable camels. The entire assembly then kneeled. A single officer remained standing with arm resting on the Southern Cross hilt of his glittering sword which was pointing to the ground and then he raised it each time the Moslem leader bowed in prayer. A sacrifice was brought forward and two sheep were slaughtered - that was not so pleasant to see, but with the cleansing of the soul, they all stood up and then remounted their camels.

The long ceremony and solemn proceedings of Shawwal Day were held between sunrise and sunset, "when the Koran was sent forth as a guidance for the people". The end of Ramadan was proclaimed at the moment when a 'reliable' eyewitness declared before the Paramount Ruler of the Faith, that the new moon had been sighted. Then, frantic howls came from the far left, outside the arena and at that moment the thrilling sight of a cavalry messenger - the 'reliable witness' - came galloping in astride an Arabian horse, decorated with all the traditional trappings floating in the breeze, charged in front of us across the arena towards the Sultan. He drew rein with a fine display of horsemanship, forelegs down to the ground kicking up the dust and came to a halt as abruptly as he had entered, to proclaim to the Spiritual Leader that "the new moon has been sighted". Dust falling in the air made a perfect finale to end this Holy ceremony.

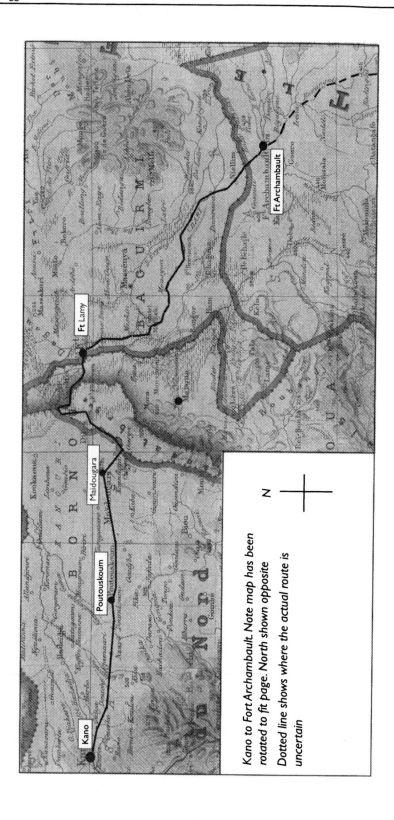

Kano to Fort Archambault. Note map has been rotated to fit page. North shown opposite

Dotted line shows where the actual route is uncertain

Progress By Perseverance
Kano To Fort Archambault

A single pair of wheel tracks left Kano, worn deep into the ground by four-wheelers. They were too wide apart for our narrow track and we went along hemmed in to the track by brown, sun dried grass about five feet high, with the motorcycle down in one groove and the sidecar up on the ridge in the middle leaning sideways at an awkward angle. Riding for many miles with the trailer like this put a strain on the front forks, besides which the physical tug of steering for hours in low gear at slow speed was tiring. Since the fibre generator drive block had worn smooth and was not driving the generator, our extra large capacity battery had been fully charged at Kano so we continued after dark using only the pilot bulb until bright moonshine sent light over the panorama and we could see better. Engine ignition was by magneto, so by not driving the generator, it saved horse-power, but gave us a meagre light only as long as it would last. We stopped during the night to let the repaired engine cool and to disconnect the unwanted rear-brake and trailer lights, when a rustling disturbance came from the tall grass near the side of us.

Immediately - if not sooner - we decided to rest somewhere else! Riding a distance of about two hundred miles still in one or other of the two deep wheel ruts, we passed native villages spread far apart on our way to Potiskum, where Hausa tribes with their livestock lived off the land. At this small town we were able to obtain local food, water and fuel. Under the thatched roof rest shelter we had a short sleep ready for another moonlight night ride.

In the half-light of dawn, Blenk's voice from the saddle stirred me. "Look - what's that? Can you see something?". "Yes," I said, after paying attention. Among the bushes on the left was a native walking towards us, following in the footsteps of an escort in front of him who was holding the end of a chain attached to an iron ring around his neck while another behind him, held the end of a chain from the back of his neck. A guard mounted on horseback kept pace with a rifle slung across his back. A United Nations Convention on the continuance of domestic slavery was still hard to implement especially in certain regions of central Africa. He could be guilty of a crime and collapse before ever reaching a tribunal to hear his case, but whatever the circumstance, it was a sad sight.

The wheel ruts here were not quite so deep as the track became more sandy. We passed by small villages at Damagum, Murbe and Damaturu. With their round huts and thatched tops they all looked alike among the trees, where natives with primitive tools were working on the land. We came in turn to the villages of Ngumdu, Beni-Sheik, Kesawa and Auno, about twenty miles apart. The track improved approaching the town of Maiduguri, about 289 miles from Kano. As yet, we had not seen another vehicle.

Maiduguri

In the distance, a cheerful sight of the British flag came into view, flying over the Embassy which resembled an old English country mansion. After three days of riding in wide apart wheel ruts and along the central ridge, we reached the Government building. The Ambassador and staff, used to the administration of gathering facts about travellers in the region, heard from Kano that we were coming. They made us welcome and invited us to stay at their residence. We enjoyed the comforts of home, the first real bathroom since Algiers and lay down to sleep, safe and sound, in beds under mosquito nets, almost too soft and comfortable! Then in the morning, like a pair of softies, we breakfasted in bed.

In the official workshop our little craft looked so tiny among the monster trucks made to withstand austere conditions, yet they too were continually being repaired. A mechanic serviced the Panther engine and did some carpentry to hold the trailer together, while we used some free time. With apologies from His and Her Excellency for having to attend a civic function that evening, they instructed the servants to care for us in their absence and invited us to stay another day or so.

That evening, domestic house-boy servants dressed in blue sashed, white duty uniforms, served a multi-course evening meal. We sat under ceiling fans at a luxuriously laid dining table all to ourselves, then we relaxed on the veranda in easy-chairs, sipped liqueur and entertained ourselves chatting about the disparities in the lives of people we had come across.

At times like this my twin emotions of Conscience and Vagabond were again in conflict. "Yes," said the Vagabond spirit in me, "stay another day or so before leaving Nigeria, go to the bank for currency to enter Chad; replenish our supplies; go to the post office, look around and see with our own eyes the slave market." The Conscience spirit within me, said, "It was more important to go on to Cape Town". A triangle, whether emotional or otherwise was according to ancient Greeks, the symbol of equilibrium, balance and harmony. The Reality spirit was a practical genie and component to my emotional triangle and this time agreed with my Vagabond emotion and turned our dilemma to stay a while longer.

The only land approach to little known Nigeria used to be from Egypt, by boat up the River Nile to reach the Ibo people. The Ibo, like anyone else, express themselves by their works of art. Only a few white people had been to where the Ibo people live in the French West Africa colony of Dahomey, to the west of Nigeria, now known as Benin. In the old glass case of my father's museum back home, were a few pieces of metalwork made long ago by the metal smiths of Benin, an artistry that has almost vanished. In the market place I caught a glimpse of a woman wearing a necklace that looked familiar and the most beautiful, simply because she had it on. Artwork was designed in wax, wet clay wrapped around it to form a mould and then dried with heat that melts away the wax inside, leaving a hard mould in which to cast the work. Molten metal, bronze or gold, is then poured into the mould and allowed to cool. The finished work of art is extracted by chipping away the clay mould, the melted wax having already been lost. This 'lost wax' process, as it is known, can never be duplicated and makes each piece an original.

Leaving Maiduguri, we continued along ruts in the track passing the villages of Giari and Mufi over a very bad stretch of road to the Nigerian customs post at Kala-Belge where we left the British colony to enter the French Equatorial colony of Chad. Passports and documents were checked by a French soldier who readily gave us clear passage with a polite reminder to ride on the right-hand side of the road!

Chad

We stopped at Kouseri village under its thatched rest-shelter in the fading daylight ready to cross the Logone River next day in daylight. The Logone and Chari Rivers come together here. Neither of these two great rivers had a bridge - it was as if we had to cross two rivers at the same time to reach Fort Lamy (later renamed N'Djamena). Both these rivers flow into Lake Chad a hundred miles north, where evaporation of the lake has been greater than the water flowing into it, leaving villages which used to be near water now five miles away. Many tributaries of two other great rivers, the Niger and the Congo flow through the vales of central Africa and none we came to had a bridge, only a ferry.

This ferry was typical of most of them, always on the other side of the river! It looked still, like a statue, with no activity over that side, causing another long delay. While manoeuvring the Panther and trailer to the exact position on the ramps leading down the river bank where the ferry would dock, the primary drive chain from the engine sprocket to gearbox, broke. We just had time before the ferry came across, to unpack and slip on a new chain. The ramps sloping down the river bank were spaced for four-wheelers and were too far apart for our narrow track, so to suit our wheels, the crew moved a ramp and we rolled down to the river bank. Worried about our brakes not being strong enough to control the load to stop us overshooting and plunging into the river off the other end of the ferry, we got all available hands to use their full strength, to hang on behind and hold us back. Lying across the Chari River bed was a draw-chain, securely anchored at both river banks. It was raised above the water by the ferry and lay fallow on deck, sliding back into the water, astern of the ferry.

To float us across the river, the crew pulled on the chain, "Heave-Ho! ... Heave-Ho!". In those days there were no outboard motors and the crew pulled together on the draw chain in a beautiful harmonious chant - a call to repel snakes and crocodiles, for wildlife will move away from any disturbance. We floated smoothly across into Fort Lamy. A ramp was moved into position to suit our wheel-track and we rode up the other side of the river to reach Chad. Fort Lamy was quite a small place. It did not appear much like a capital city and seat of Government, especially at noon when everything was closed. I asked a French maid serving at an outside table, under a canopy where well dressed people were seated, "please may we have some water ?". From inside a building, she kindly gave us water, not knowing how much we appreciated a drink of plain, clean, cold water as of course there were no refrigerators or ice cubes, and added "you may have the remainder of some rabbit stew."

Along the next three hundred and eighty miles across the vast southern plain of Chad, there were only four widely spaced villages on the way to Fort Archambault (later renamed Sarh) and this was a good place for us to check everything again very carefully. Blenk and myself so very much needed new footwear and this would be the best place to buy tropical jack boots (snake boots) hand made by local craftsmen - there being no manufactured goods. Soon, every merchant around knew we wanted to buy some boots. One of them actually came to the rest hut with all kinds of leather work, belts and bags of well-made handicraft. An old trick typically used on a white customer when peddling something for sale, was to double the price, so according to their own way of doing business, we would buy from the one who offered us a good pair of knee-length boots at the lowest price. Twenty-four hours after we began to look for boots and when they thought we were getting ready to leave, two pairs made by a Sara leather worker who we had our eyes on, came down to a fair price.

Our quilted and lead-foil lined topee headwear were inclined to be heavy, but none the worse for wear gave maximum protection from the sun and together with spine-pads and dark glasses made us as sun proof as possible. Within the equatorial belt, radiation from the sun was cast straight down. Even on a cloudy day it was more harmful than in northern and southern latitudes where slanting rays, although directly overhead at noon, were not so penetrating. For a few minutes I took off my helmet to look between the Panther and sidecar to inspect the new primary chain for stretch and adjustment, when an aide-de-camp from the rest hut came over to me and, indicating with finger to head, implied 'put on your helmet!'. Meanwhile, the French people with whom we had now become acquainted, wanted to have a send-off party for us. They arranged that the motorcycle and trailer would be taken across the Chari River on the ferry in daylight, before the crew ended their 'Heave-Ho' at dusk and remain on the dismal track on the other side of the river leading to Fort Archambault with a policeman to guard it. Blenk and myself would then be taken across after the social gathering in a *perogue*, a hollowed out tree-trunk, in the darkness of the night and they would bring back the policeman waiting there.

At sunset, a long narrow table, made up of anything to serve the purpose, stood under withered trees. On sandy ground was spread with a white cloth and laid for about sixteen people, including two Germans who had checked in at the rest shelter. In candle-light and with dance music by gramophone, we heard languages we did not understand, not knowing what to make of all the foreign chatter, but which conveyed meanings of goodwill, which we understood very well. The most important part was not the food, but the *esprit de corps*. I thought, "how else, but for the motorcycle, was it possible to have this cheerful time in such a dismal place?"

After the party, the boatman in the *perogue* was waiting to paddle Blenk and me across the river to where our motorcycle stood parked. Soldiers gave a salute followed by less formal friendly waves from the others as we drifted away to the rhythm of mellow chants to warn wildlife to move away as the oars cut the shiny black water. We kept our hands well clear of the sides of the boat, for whether by day or by night, there were reptiles, crocodiles and hopefully, only docile hippos about. The policeman guarding our motorcycle was asleep in the sidecar; he was aroused and taken back to Fort Lamy. We were alone.

Brown, sun dried grasses five feet high and fallen trees cleared for the passage of vehicles, lay by the rutted track as we made headway, in pitch darkness alongside the Chari River at about fifteen miles an hour. Until the generator, which had stopped charging the battery could some day be repaired, the extra capacity battery in the sidecar had again been recharged, but the dim pilot-bulb made night riding difficult. Wildlife roamed, mosquitoes, snakes and other living creatures came to the river under cover of darkness to drink, making our ride as hazardous by night as in the tropical sun's rays by day. But either way we felt safer from dangerous creepy-crawlies wearing our new knee length boots. Neither the air-cooled engine nor ourselves could endure long spells of tropical humid heat, as the folk at home had tried to explain to us. The rainy season would soon turn the hot, sun-baked track into impassable deep mud.

In daylight a pair of cubs ran out of the grass onto the track in front of us, rolling over each other playing, mauling each other's head and tail. We stopped, as wildlife has the right-of-way and the young felines were fascinating to watch. Ending their frolic they bounced away in opposite directions giving no clue where their lair would be. If they were leopards, the most fierce of cats, the female was never far away and would attack to defend them.

At the next wayside rest shelter, fatigue had the upper hand and we stopped to rest. The poles of this shelter were too close together to get the trailer under thatched cover so we camped outside wasting no time putting up the mosquito net. We lit a fire to ward off prowling wildlife, agreeing to take turns to stoke the flickering flame of our guardian light. In the morning the heap of cold ash looked as if the night-fire had burned itself out a long time ago. Who let the fire-light go out last night? But, in a place like this, it not worth having an argument about it.

Ruts in the track were deeper and the central ridge was steeper, and having little ground clearance, the sidecar chassis scraped along the ridge. Like Tweedle Dum and Tweedle Dee, moving from one side up and then that side down, almost all the way since leaving Kano, it put a strain on the steering and the front forks until eventually, after about another hundred miles we had trouble.

Disaster

We stopped to adjust a few wheel spokes and tried to correct the egg-shaped rim of the warped front wheel, but after a short distance of successive kangaroo hops, the wheel-hub finally broke free from the brake drum and the whole front wheel collapsed. Unlike other breakdowns, this time it was impossible to coax another inch out of her, not even if we tried to push.

Darkness soon blotted out everything. Blenk, as usual was straight to the point, neither stressing or minimising the catastrophe. "The wheels are not interchangeable. We've spare spokes, axles and bearings" I said slowly, trying not to lose courage and feel doomed, "but no hub." Blenk fingered the broken pieces, "how often does anything come this way?". "About once a week", I murmured adding as an after thought, " the mail left Fort Lamy just before we did." We laid on the trailer, not daring to sleep, listening with strained ears for something to come along. Too hot to be hungry, moving around was an effort and of little use until we got up in the morning, when at most, we changed positions from lying upon the trailer under mosquito net, to lying on sleeping bags down on the ground. We spent the time listening and waiting for a vehicle, that did not come. Tools lay around. We were startled by rustling in the long grass, but it was only a native going down to the river to fish. The whole day passed by, but nothing else. Blenk moaned with a grievance, "we may have to cool our heels here for six days," and wiping the sweat off my nose, I told her in a low voice, "my heels won't cool here."

We stayed stuck in a wheel rut alongside the Chari River. Food was scarce, and unclean river water had to be boiled, but that did nothing to improve the taste. We did not discuss the situation. At night, we could hear faint roars and splashes of animals prowling down by the river. The second night I could sense Blenk's restless activity so I asked her "how much nearer to Cape Town are we tonight than yesterday ?". She evaded the question, but asked, "how does one treat a jigger flea? I think there is one in my toe". That settled the matter by making us both get up. Jigger fleas must be attended to immediately; when a parasite gets under the skin to lay eggs, if left too long, serious infection will occur.

In the miraculous way that news travels when there is no apparent means of communication, two youths from one of the few-and-far-between villages came to see what had sprung up in the night, and looked at us in bewilderment. Their Chief wanted to know 'why white man hang around?' In the soothing balm of the evening, we walked about half a mile to a village of round thatched huts. The Chief, a six-foot giant of ebony, received us with a dignified bow and spoke in the lingo of the Sara people. We understood him only by his expression and outstretched hands. His Eminence seemed to regret our plight as our situation was hourly becoming more precarious. He tried to help, and to show his concern, he told a tribesman to escort us back to the forlorn motorcycle. We were suddenly enveloped in darkness, for the nearer to the equator, the shorter the twilight. The 'boy', which means a native of any age, took a smouldering branch of wood from a fire to probe the path ahead like a mine-detector as snakes and wildlife fear smell of smoke or fire. At his waist hung a hatchet and he walked steadfastly in front of us to lead the way. He stayed to light our camp fire and took another glowing stick to probe his way safely back through the bush and return to the village.

Fortunately our wheel trouble happened at no great distance from one of the four villages in this sparsely populated plain of Chad. In the morning a tribesman came from the village to bring us some goats milk and some eggs and in addition, the Chief sent his respects by way of a few small cakes baked from mealie flour. They were very light and spongy, as good as the best made by one of his wives and also some local honey. The honey had self-refined, as the sand, ants and dead flies had all settled at the bottom of the jar. That night we heard hippo in the river grunting to their satisfaction just like they do in the zoo, then they sink unpredictably to churn up the muddy water.

During the day, a native fishing, came up the river-bank and we swapped a measure of tea for four of his catch. Conversation between Blenk and me was about anything except intimation of defeat, although slow progress and adversity strained my perseverance, but being enthusiastic, the thought of reaching Cape Town never left us so we resorted to "Hobson's Choice" - and waited. I knew one day something would come along.

That evening the dreadful tedium of waiting for a vehicle to come along was breached by some local drama, when the same tribesman from the village returned to our breakdown site. In his hand he held a flute-like whistle. He was accompanied by two other able-bodied tribesmen wearing their native negligee. One would stay by the motorcycle in the dark to intercept any vehicle that happened to pass by, and the other two natives were guides to take us for a walk through the shrubs and stretch our legs after three days of idleness. The man to walk in front of us, took a smouldering branch of brush wood from our fire to repel snakes to clear the ground ahead. All wildlife can be kept at bay by smell, sound or showing a light.

Here and there he touched a tuft of growth with his smouldering branch of firewood, careful not to start a bush fire, as we walked in single file behind. From his waist hung a hard crotch-like part of a tree as a knob-end club to throw with deadly aim. The man who walked behind us blew his three-hole whistle all the while sounding a penetrating long-winded wail to alert wildlife to move away by fear of noise - but they would still attack if suddenly frightened. While we were walking, villagers came over to our breakdown spot to be with their sentinel 'boy' while waiting to halt anyone who may come along. As we returned from our walk, they began to dance - leaping, foot-stamping and 'jitter-bugging' to the beat of tom-toms. Nobody danced like these Africans.

A tom-tom and some of their handicraft, were to be admired in my childhood home, but the lovely part of their culture and their dancing, remained with them. I listened to the rhythm of their drums - not a mechanical beat - and could see their graceful profile in the darkness. I sat astride the motorcycle and switched on the headlamp to shed light on them and watched with special interest more than just their dancing. It was the joy of the coming together of blacks and whites on friendly terms. I had never really been sure about this before, but perhaps after all, Jazz roots may have originated in places like this rather then in New Orleans or south-side Chicago.

No matter how well their domestic animals were protected, the presence of a village attracted lions after easy prey. We heard the mellow roar of night prowlers somewhere close by ready for their night kill - midges also found their way through the mosquito net for a night feed making sleep out of the question. Clothes came to feel like garments of hair and I could have renounced my soul for a bath, feeling fagged, under-nourished and over-stressed as if in some other world beyond the pale of civilisation. In this low-lying region of Chad, cited as the 'White man's grave', I was about ready to put up a white flag to surrender, wanting nothing more than to get away from here alive.

Rescued

Another dawn, another sunrise. At last the sound of something coming gave a boost to my frame of mind. We scrambled to our feet to see a truck coming our way, but my fickle mood soon changed and sank right down to the bottom of my new boots. Already it looked so very much overladen - how can it possibly carry anything more? The French driver stopped and I will not forget his surprise when he first saw us stuck there. Apparently this place was half way from Fort Lamy. Fort Archambault was another one hundred and eighty miles away. There were two passengers seated in front next to the driver, and at the back of the truck with merchandise, baggage, a cargo of sugar, pick and shovel and an excess of other things, two porters held grimly on. Front seats were made available for Blenk and myself as their code of ethics was respectively adhered to. There was no hard feeling, except a tinge of my conscience as the two Greek passengers went behind with the Arab porters. The trailer with all our possessions, was hitched behind the truck as we left having dragged the motorcycle under a bush without its front wheel. We took with us the broken wheel pieces to be welded together intending to hitch a lift back to this bush with the repaired front wheel and get the Panther rolling again.

The truck fitted into the ruts and we went along easily with the trailer rolling along behind, tilted one wheel up on the ridge in the middle of the track. The men at the back kept an eye on it.

"By Jove!" I thought, if we could go along like this all the way to Cape Town.... but then, the challenge of our expedition would no longer be possessed. We stopped at a wayside thatched shelter in the heat of midday and by late afternoon were back on the track. The next time the truck stopped was when we reached the Bahr River - there was no bridge. I woke up in a dark, tropical humid atmosphere. Honking their horn and flicking the headlights, aroused the natives living in huts on the other side. It seemed every ferry we ever came to was always on the opposite side of a river. One by one the crew of the raft stirred to man the ferry and came over this side to float us across. The raft was not big enough to carry both the truck and our trailer at the same time, so we all went over with the truck on the first crossing and had to wait for the crew to go back and fetch the trailer. Landing on the south side of the Bahr River, the rutted track was just as bad. We moved along very well fitting into the ruts with tall brown sun dried grass on either side and the trailer taking the strain as it was tilted by the centre ridge, hoping to reach Fort Archambault before the weather changed. The weather was causing some anxiety. A storm which was following us, made the sky look dark with peals of thunder coming closer.

Torrential rain

Near another village we came to yet another river without a bridge and had the same problem of not enough room on the raft for both the truck and the trailer, so it took twice as long to get across. Up stream the storm had already set in causing the river here to rise rapidly. A squall from a sudden change of temperature sent leaves, sand and dust spiralling into the air with images of trees swaying in the wind like those graceful tom-tom dancers alongside the river. In mid-stream, the ferry was making the second crossing bringing over our trailer and possessions and precious wheel pieces when the current suddenly increased to a torrent which tried to swept the raft away. I worried about ever seeing our things again. The crew had difficulty keeping the raft on course. We watched helplessly and heard their frantic shouts to each other as the exhausted gang managed to paddle the heavy raft to anchor up safely at the landing ramps.

The trailer was hastily attached to the truck. The driver drove at a slow pace to another little river with an unsafe looking plank bridge which had been cautiously rolled over it ahead of the storm. He steered towards Fort Archambault as rain began to pour on the mud track and stopped outside an Indian trading post where everyone rushed inside out of the rain, leaving Blenk, myself and the cargo of sugar out in a deluge. We covered their merchandise with our ground-sheet, looking like a pair of mermaids. The two Greeks and Arab porters vanished before our fate would be decided.

The Seymour Mission

We were driven along a private dirt road between mango trees to a Mission station where a ranch-style veranda overlooking a desert-scape garden, had a welcoming appearance. Missionaries were the first outsiders to come here from the civilised world to help primitive people in Africa, educate natives in remote places, teach hygiene and how to cultivate the land for better crops. They also expounded the Gospel. The Seymour evangelists in this part of Chad were Americans on a two year assignment of field duty; they had their two young children with them. The Seymour Mission was an influential place around here. The sizable house, with its spare rooms, had a complete set-up for communal activities. The pathway around the grounds led to the chapel, school building and medical ward. For the first time we now met Americans, known for their hospitality and their easy-going English-French-Sanka-tribal dialect, which solved our language difficulty with such a kind and hearty welcome, that we left our plight with the broken wheel to be thought out later.

The nearest place where welding could be done to rebuild the hub, brake drum and our broken wheel, was at Bangui, the capital of the neighbouring French Equitoria colony of Ubangi Chari, more than four hundred and fifty miles away. The mail truck on its routine run from here, would take some time to return with the rebuilt front wheel.

Local transport was by *push*, a chair mounted on a bicycle wheel. Shafts secured to the armrests, extending fore-and-aft like a Chinese rickshaw, as porters within the shafts, one in front and the other behind. They rolled Blenk and myself, holding the broken pieces in our arms while seated in our chairs, half a mile or so to the post office. We were made to feel most welcome to stay at the Mission while we waited the return of our wheel.

The Fort Lamy road formed a T-junction here, the left turn leading to military barracks important enough to have its own small air strip; the right turn leading to the Mission post, market place, hotel, several shops and French government and post offices, all clustered around a few trees. Except for the doctor's family, military personnel and Greek trucking merchant, Blenk and I were the only white people and after a while staying at the Mission, we came to adjust to the African conditions. Travellers passing through sometimes made a courtesy visit to the Missionary and we often met their guests. One day a well-known American film crew called in on their way to the Belgian Congo to film pygmies in the Itrui Forest and record primitive lifestyle and tribal customs, lest their way of life faded in this changing world. Their assignment included an elephant hunt and if possible to film the capture of a wild elephant. They gave us the exact location of their base and told us they had seen our forlorn motorcycle. They told us it was alright and that a letter had been tied to the handlebar. In an undeveloped colony protected mainly by a primitive code of probity, we were pleased to know it was quite safe where we had left it under a bush.

A dictionary of words spoken by the Sara people, was already being compiled as later in the year, a Conference of Missionaries was to be held at the Seymour Mission. While delayed here, we assisted in putting together a combination of unwritten sounds of Sara language. Africa has no particular language and communicates in more than a thousand tongues. Along the banks of the Chari and provincial rivers, terra-cotta and bronze relics of a mediaeval culture had been discovered and a few were on display.

To cool the room where we worked, a door was suspended from the ceiling, hung on it's hinges and free to swing back and forth like an Indian *punkah*. A string tied to the door-knob pulled by a house-boy sitting on the floor, leaning against the wall, kept it swinging with pendulum-like tempo. These long spells of weariness often led him to nod in boredom. One afternoon a black mamba snake, the most venomous of all snakes, lying up on the rafters, slipped and fell to the ground. The frightened snake coiled itself ready to jump unpredictably from here to there around the floor - the moments that followed were very 'exciting'. The punkah-boy leapt to his feet and with the stick he carried, caught the snake in mid-air as it jumped, to strike the fatal blow, breaking its back and render it harmless. The house-boy's skill and courage proved to us that after all, he was not so dull. We found these people to be heart-rich, feeling and compassionate. Everything I could assimilate from these impoverished natives, in this harsh and undeveloped land, unabashedly added to my own education. I wish we could have spoken to them in their tribal tongue.

One day a commotion started on the Mission campus when a local resident discovered his bicycle had been stolen and accused a Mission classman of stealing it. Court was set up in the classroom; the Judge who heard the case was the preacher. Primitive folk have their own moral code and they are inclined to associate education and wealth with 'white man's culture'. During the proceedings the accused Mission lad confessed to the Judge that he had never thought of 'stealing' until he had read of it in the Ten Commandments - 'Thou shalt not steal'.

River crossing

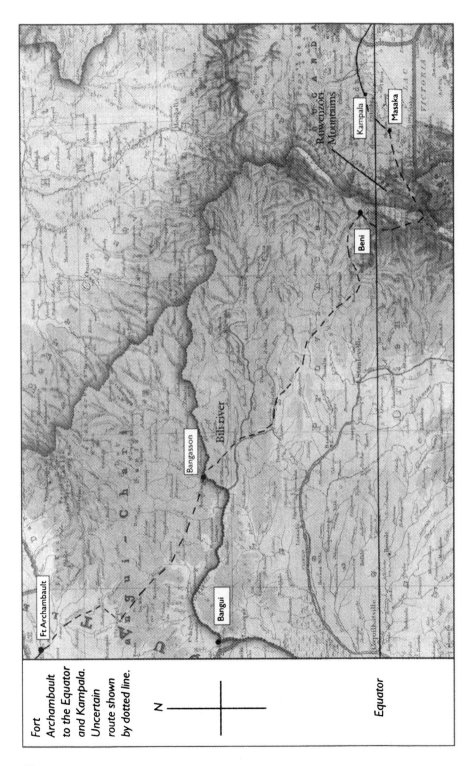

Fort Archambault to the Equator and Kampala. Uncertain route shown by dotted line.

N

Equator

Towards The Equator
Fort Auchambault To The Equator

The mail truck returned from Bangui with our rebuilt front wheel in good shape and having recovered the deserted Panther, we were ready on April 19th, to roll towards the equator. The letter tied to the handlebar was written in French by Swiss travellers, greeting us and wishing us 'Good Luck'. They had read in a European newspaper about our expedition.

In a memorable moment, we said farewell to the evangelists who had been good friends and expressed our gratitude for their help in our predicament, finding it hard to break away. They were also sad to see us leave. All we could do was to smile, shake hands and say 'Thank You!' Leaving the Mission we passed the air-strip barracks and we again saw the soldiers we met at the garage, with their trucks, and they beckoned us to join them for *l'aperitif* before going on.

It was mid-night when we finally left! The border between the colonies of Chad and Ubangui-Chari was not marked, but if anything had come along, the rule of the road remained the same. A sudden rain shower drenched us before we could reach our waterproofs, packed inside the trailer, but our thin clothes dried almost instantly in this climate. The rainy season would soon change the hard sun-baked mud track into a morass, and then we would be stuck in mud, instead of sand. Only on a motorcycle, without a cockpit or windscreen, could we sniff the aroma of fresh green growth, glittering wet, and feel warm rain falling a few thousand feet above the parched lower plain of Chad as well as come to close quarters with the splendour of tropical Africa. Perhaps a little too close - "Wal, turn round - look back!", said Blenk from the saddle. I quickly turned myself around in the sidecar, and looking forward saw a huge snake coiled on the narrow track in our way, camouflaged by it's mottle marks, difficult to see until almost running into it. Unable to stop, Blenk dared to squeeze past hoping, Heaven forbid, it would not move. I was glad she did not see it sooner rather than later. Neither of us knew much about snakes, but Blenk said afterwards she thought it was a python, so enormous and heavy-bodied it could have stretched out to be about ten feet long and taken forever to move.

On the way to Bangassou, we came to another geophysical phenomenon similar to that previously encountered like a roller coaster in an amusement park. It was not so amusing however, as the lack of engine power on the way to the top of each hummock had us grind to a stop. The best way to get the feel of an engine is by riding a motorcycle. The knack was for us to jump off at the right moment and wedge a handy rock behind the rear wheel to prevent it rolling backwards. Into bottom gear with both of us pushing and then, with enough speed, hop on board as we had so often done, we dashed over and down with enough impetus to climb to the top of another. We were getting good at this. Three hundred miles into this sparsely populated colony, or about half way to Bangassou, we stopped at a wayside shelter. A Sara tribal village of thatched round huts lay in the background. Our staple food now was rice, as here there was plenty of water to cook it and unlike bread, it did not go stale; it could be rinsed clean when grubby and it was manageable to carry. We also had time to prepare it.

The Congo

The other half of the route, in contrast to rocks, sand, parched land, was a wet ride up the Des Bondos hills of tropical scenery, near the border of the Belgian Congo. In the pretty little border town of Bangassou, a friendly English speaking Norwegian family lived in a brick house. They came to say hello and invited us to stay a night with them. They were a great help with our neglected trailer housekeeping and attached to the motorcycle, a list of things to do.

Customs checked us out of French Equatoria and we entered the Belgian Congo riding fifty miles to the Belgian customs along a good strip of earth road. About half way along, we had to ferry across the Ubangui river. The camera crew we met at the mission post in Chad a few weeks ago had already passed through customs and thoughtfully left a message that we were coming on our way to Cape Town, so they checked our passports and let us continue without collecting tariff on camera or firearms.

Rain drenched the countryside and turned the hard sunbaked-mud track, which had little or no sand and gravel, into a quagmire. The equator was another thousand miles away. As we passed Bantu villages of thatched beehive-shaped huts, our wheels rolled where natives trod a twisty path along otherwise impenetrable forest. It was a magnificent preamble into Jungle country. This was 'Black Africa'.

We were now in a hot, humid climate and in one of the few remaining places where animal and plant life were left alone to keep alive the balance of nature. Primitive people such as the pygmies integrated with nature. As we were riding through the Ituri forest, we heard bird calls, the chatter of primates and saw wildlife which to us was so unfamiliar and too prolific to grasp in a short time. it was like seeing words written on a page, but not being able to understand the story line.

The jungle

Although only on the northern edge of the jungle, the vegetation was beyond my imagination with leaves so thick the sun could not penetrate. Trees a hundred and fifty feet tall had vines clinging to them up to the topmost branches, striving for light, as they arched over, coming together high above our heads and shutting out the daylight. We rode with the headlight switched on through what was known as 'Darkest Africa'. It usually rained for several hours at the same time every day. Only a little rain came through the canopy of thick leaves to fall on us below and any strange sound aroused wildlife. Several times a snake came out right in front of us without a chance of us avoiding running over it, but only once did we look back to see it lying motionless on the track behind. At other times they were nowhere to be seen. As when Blenk was too scared to stop for that python earlier, in fear of it tangling itself around us, she still feared stopping again.

In those days any kind of mechanisation was unknown here. The only means of transport was by porters. Usually we saw only a few porters, but once we saw about fifty natives walking in single file. Their graceful gait was almost as if floating along. Barefoot, they were carrying loads of cotton harvest on their heads to a river-boat ten miles away. It has been said, "The best way to see Africa - in fact the only way to see it in a single lifetime - is for a private pilot to travel a great deal by air ... having spotted something that looks interesting, descend for a clearer view or come down at the nearest airstrip to satisfy one's curiosity".

However, nobody could ever meet natives or see wildlife better than we did through-out the course of our motorcycle ride to Cape Town. Unlike many other places, Africa's shallow ocean-washed coast-line is not endowed with natural harbours or ports for deep-sea ships to dock and much of Africa has been inaccessible for trade with some seafaring nations. The Sahara desert seals off access to the interior of the continent. Other countries advanced a long time ago by building roads and railways to ports where deep sea ships could moor, but for centuries central Africa slumbered for lack of communication with the outside world. The awakening occurred with the advent of military, civil and commercial aviation. The era of long-distance flights from industrial countries to inland airports rather than seaports, of a formerly inaccessible continent has brought about this uncustomary maturation of Africa's development, from the interior outwards. Uncivilised tribes previously beyond reach, now are compelled to catch up, no longer by living in a colony, but by advancing to their own independent nations in a rapidly changing world.

We reached the Bili River. Bantu boatmen from one of about two hundred or so ethnic tribes in the Congo ferried us across on a raft, but without a detailed map of the African interior, finding our way by reading information typed out onto paper, was like looking for clues in a treasure hunt. Directions would read as follows:-

'Leave by left-hand fork marked 'Bondo'; In 10 mile, ferry across Bili River 72m; Bondo (Hotel; petrol 4 frs/litre; garage, repairs by favour of Marco Company); Leave by ferry road. Cross this (Uele River) a second time 20m later. Likati (River) and a third time over the same river 8m onward; through forest country. Another ferry 80m further in 117m from Bondo. Buta 130m (Hotel, bank, petrol 3.60/litre, repairs). River Ituri ferry. In 4m branch right, (it may be advisable to continue ahead to Irumu for 12m for accommodation, petrol, stores); Road passes through

Ituri Forest with pygmie tribes; Moora pygmie village 65m; Beni - Total 300 miles. Magnificent view of Ruwenzori Glaciers.'

In the small town of Buta, at the very centre of the continent, the weather was dry, the earth road was wide, hard and smooth and there actually were telephone poles along the main thoroughfare. In seven days we had come a thousand miles and stopped here to look around and service the motorcycle. It seemed a person of any nationality Asian, European or Western who could read, write and grapple with daily affairs, was owner or manager of a small business. The exception was a native endowed with the cult of the ethnic group and the skill of a craft, seldom given the opportunity to progress in their own land. Native artistry made abstract creations of human and animal figures carved in black ebony and white ivory, as distinctive to the eye as the sound of tom-tom to the ear.

Equatorial evenings brought sudden darkness and a thunderstorm loomed in the distance, where a traveller's thatched roof cover in Buta proved a convenient shelter for the night. The next two hundred and fifty miles had eighteen rivers, without bridges to cross. Some were more than a half mile wide, but not as difficult or time consuming as the little rivers in isolated places, where the raft crew were not well prepared. Bantu boatmen paddled us across the wide Ituri river. As the blades of their oars dipped into the water, their deep-toned voices chanted our approach to warn off hippos and crocodile, which move away from danger. Yet to me, the rhythm of the shanty conveyed an exciting sense of 'adventure in music', which without the means to record them, those melodious river crossings remain just a memory.

Thunder boomed further away and we looked for shelter on the other side of the river. Along the way on the left, we came to a cluster of cone-shaped huts in a gloomy-looking quadrant, but there was no thatched shelter for us tonight. The sound of our motorcycle stirred the village. A Hunde tribesman, in a ragged white shirt, held a smouldering branch taken from the night fire - no one will step into the darkness without protection of a smoke-smelling and glowing live ember. He was followed by others who had never seen a motorcycle, nor possibly white women. I had some qualms about this place where 'civilised' custom had not penetrated so deep into the Congo, that just now the thought of cannibals crossed my mind. The tribesman started our fire in a strong wind as the thunder hovered around.

Pygmies

The next day at increasing altitude, (latitude 0.55°N) we slowly approached the equator and that night the thunderstorm set in. We laid in our sleeping bags listening to the wind blowing and the rain falling, expecting the tent to be blown down at any minute. Flashes of lightning lasted long enough to flood-light trees swaying in the squall like natives dancing to tom-toms of thunder. Rain was falling as if looking through a sheet of frosted glass. A hearty gust of wind wafted

Blenk with the Pygmi people

everything laying outside all over the place. The storm drifted away and we scurried around our jungle patch, collecting up scattered belongings. The only thing that had gone was the soap which we picked up further away than wind could have carried it; it bore distinct fang or claw marks, deeply indented.

A letter in our briefcase, hand-written by a Greek trader in Buta, introducing us to a tribe of Pygmies in the Ituri Forest and to Chief Bondo, of the village of Ekibondo, his wives and the Witch Doctor. Pygmies are some of the most primitive people on earth. They are shy and hide from strangers. It would be interesting to seek out these fifty-four inch tall Bambuti inhabitants, near to the Moora village and pay them a visit. Slowly climbing to higher elevation nearer the equator, we came to a fork in the track and stopped to check the direction to follow. This aroused our 'emotional triangle' - the spirits of Conscience, Vagabond and Reality. Leading contender was Conscience, that we should not go off the route again because if we accepted these invitations and deviations, we would never get to Cape Town, besides the distance of another twenty-five miles or so into the interior and back to this fork in the track was too much for the already over-worked motorcycle. As for ourselves, we still had some very hard days ahead.

On the other hand Vagabond wanted to become acquainted with a Witch Doctor in the depth of the African jungle, just as much a part of our expedition, and it would be a marvellous experience for us to see the pygmies and not fret about saving time and mileage.

The Reality genie agreed with Vagabond and we conceded that it would be madness, but put to good use. So, in harmonious agreement we went in the direction of Ekibondo to see the pygmies.

No longer having a working odometer, speedometer or timepiece, we estimated the time and distance to reach the tribe, being careful not to get lost in the jungle. If it lead nowhere and there was no trace of the pygmies, we would be prudent and turn back. Of course Conscience would say, "serves you right; you should have taken my advice."

Ekibondo was a crudely trimmed compound of thatched round huts raised off the ground on low-level stilts. At the sound of our motorcycle, everyone disappeared except Chief Bondo himself. The fearsome figure stood there alone and accepted our letter of introduction. He could not read, so a loud-voiced call beckoned a henchman who could read. This tribesman, of fine physique and clad in loincloth, with shiny black skin and tribal body scars, came to read the letter out loud to the Chief. What a strange tongue! The Chief had thought at first our letter was a message of war from white man, but tension turned to joy and then we became his distinguished guests. His rallying call brought inhabitants back into the compound. At first they all looked alike until we could tell one from another. A hut was made available to us and when the Chief noticed how many times we stepped up and down the rungs in and out of the hut to the trailer, he ordered men to lift it up inside, but his good intention gave me a feeling of captivity for having to depend on them to get out again. Helpers brought firewood and cooked our rice and we spent a day with the pygmies, but they feared the camera and turned away when we tried to take pictures. Pygmies hiding in the flora were more on the defensive than ourselves, but when Blenk opened our little cotton bag of gift trinkets from a London six-penny store we got better acquainted. The hand-out for them was a magic light - a red bicycle reflector for the bravest one whose outstretched hand came, close enough to take it.

The forest provides the pygmies will all their essential needs. Fibres from trees are spun into thread for sewing and weaving cloth. Leaves are used to thatch their huts. Some leaves have medicinal value; other plants bear fruit and nuts. Pygmies can distinguish wholesome and medicinal plants from harmful poisonous ones in a way that a pharmacist could not do without analysis. Spears, bows and arrows for hunting are used to kill meat off the land, fowl from the air and fish from the river for food, and when these basic tools are poisoned the pygmies can very well defend themselves.

A strange sight was to see their water-melon shaped heads. The head of a baby, bound with twine, will in time grow elongated which this tribe consider to be beautiful. This was one of about two hundred pygmie tribes in the Congo, each with different dialects.

Daylight faded and a huge bonfire was aglow to the beat of tom-toms, when the Witch Doctor used his magical power to perform a tribal dance of fantastic leaps, to the weirdest yowls at the flames, supposedly to influence the

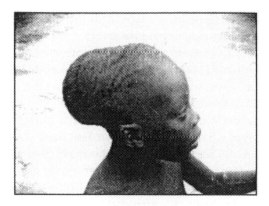

Bambuti child with elongated head

Spirit and make a person good or evil. The voodoo act in the Ituri forest was surely one of the world's last primitive ceremonial rites of it's kind. This, I said to myself - this, is my idea of a real birthday party, for today it really was my birthday, 30th April.

We prepared to leave at dawn. Chief Bondo gave instructions for helpers not to be late in the morning, for on a dull day when the sun does not shine, they don't get up 'because it looks too early'.

Chief Bondo presented himself in bright coloured bird feathers, wearing hand-made emblems for self-esteem and expressed his graciousness by giving us a live fowl in a hand-woven reed basket to take with us that we could hang on the back of the trailer. In acknowledgement, Blenk presented Chief Bondo with our eight-inch chrome safety-pin off our laundry bag showing him how to open and close it and its many uses. He was intrigued. Ekibondo villagers bowed to the ground as we waved good-bye and rode back to that fork in the track. Many times people asked us how we got along with the natives.

These dwarf people have been nomads of the jungle for thousands of years, worshipping guardian Spirits and speaking unwritten languages like many wild and woolly ethnic groups. Like many remote parts of the world, sooner or later with the advent of aviation, satellites and computers, we will reach and encroach upon them in the name of progress, making them catch up with the outside world. Never again will one be able to experience my idea of sheer adventure.

Elephants

Further south, natives with rakes and shovels were working to clear away fallen trees and rubble after a herd of elephants had gone by. Although quite gentle and intending no harm, elephants will reach up and eat the best leaves at the top of small trees and push them over to get what they want. The track here was made by migrating big game as they rummage for food, slowly moving along. We had just missed them, so surely we were better to be lucky than rich.

Something had to be done before long with the chicken from Ekibondo, still trapped in the basket, hanging behind the trailer. We stopped at a village for natives to prepare it ready to cook. In mime language we tried to explain what we wanted someone to do, but did not make ourselves understood, for they simply put it back in the basket alive, without any feathers on. At that Blenk promptly handed out the hatchet to finish the job.

The film crew we met at the Mission in Chad four weeks ago and a thousand miles back, were in this region. They suggested we find them here. "One of these days," I said, "we will cross the equator", but this experience was too good to miss. A herd of elephants was on the move about the time we arrived and they were ready to film the hunt and capture of a wild elephant without use of present-day animal tranquillisers. In their house after dark, lamps were placed everywhere. Access was through a doorway (or window) which was not firmly closed in case of leopards. The dogs were safely shut in and we were told about how they escaped a leopard attack. We had heard of the same danger elsewhere. Time and time again, leopards have been known to crouch on the branches of trees and leap from overhead to attack quite large prey and then disappear like a streak of lightening.

In other places too, we had been warned of the danger of wildlife at night without the protection of a light. Our headlight had reflected something like eyes in a tree - Blenk came to this conclusion by asking, "is that what they were?". In a typical cross-country vehicle, with the use of two monitors or older well-trained elephants, the hunters took us slowly into the Ituri Forest and reached a roving herd to film the capture of a wild elephant. Pygmies being natural hunters, tracked their prey against the wind, for elephants have a keen sense of smell. They singled out a healthy-looking calf and stalked the baby elephant, undetected by the herd. It would have a good up-bringing and be trained for its future role to work log-hauling or in cotton fields. The monitor elephants, one on each side, gradually moved closer then ropes were slung across from one to the other without the captive in between, becoming aware of it's plight until it was too late. Unable to resist, it was shackled and forcibly restrained between two powerful keepers and marshalled away from the herd.

For some time to come it would live and feed in it's natural environment, harnessed between two monitor elephants, for it may take weeks to reach the elephant farm. It could lay down to sleep, but the monitor elephants sleep standing up as their tusks weigh about a hundred and sixty pounds each, and if they laid down it is too difficult for them to get up again. The farm where a captured elephant was taken was an unusual looking place. Solid columns were erected to teach 'Jumbo' to walk around, turn left and right circles and to zig-zag. Arched bridges, not attached to anything, taught the elephant to walk under and on others with steps, to walk up, cross over a ditch or shuffle down the other side, each leading nowhere. A pit or deep ditch was used to learn the command 'Stop!'. All this schooling was used to identify, discipline and obey and if blessed with an especially gentle temperament, the elephant would even learn tricks to perform at a circus.

To the Equator

On 2nd May, 1935, we went off in the direction of Watsa, towards the equator. During the day, we unavoidably rolled over several more snakes than had run onto the track, but another had second sight and went the other way. The route twisted and turned, climbing steeply to a high altitude as the jungle thinned. In places we had to run alongside in bottom gear to steer and push together as we had done so many times before, to coax the motorcycle up the hill. High altitude and cool temperature affected the carburettor of the single cylinder Panther engine and for some unknown reason, the float-needle broke and fuel came streaming out of the float bowl. I whittled another float-needle out of wood from a twig with patience; it worked to a certain extent and sufficed until something better could be done.

Watsa[1], with its railway station, was the biggest place we had come to for a long time. It had new brick houses and glass shop windows and our travel-worn appearance attracted the curiosity of folk who happened to look our way. English people from the neighbouring British colony of Uganda, spoke to us and invited us to their home for a day.

The Ruwenzori Mountain range, so close to the equator yet capped with snow, stands along the border between Congo and Uganda and on the Congo side we climbed and looked down on the Ituri forest where we had been for the past week or so, to see the carpet of green trees converge with the blue sky on the horizon. When Missionary-explorer David Livingstone trekked his hazardous way here, not once was it recorded that he was fortunate enough to see all three highest peaks of the Ruwenzori Mountains at the same time. They can only be seen a few days a year when one or another is not obscured by mist, yet on the day we cast eyes along the range all three snow covered peaks, Mt Margherita, Mt Albert and Mt Stanley, Lake Edward and in the back-ground to the north, Lake Albert. A permanent 14,000 ft snow line was clearly visible.

Off again, the narrow track descended to lower altitude. In contrast we were always on the lookout, but now we had no out-look as we were flanked by elephant grass, fifteen feet high, obstructing our view. A private, well-made road near Beni, went through gold mining stratum and at the stone-built farm we asked permission to ride the short-cut on their property rather than the long way around the public route to reach the Kabasha Plateau.

---

[1] *Theresa clearly states Watsa, in her manuscript and it being on a railway line. This is clearly incorrect. Watsa is quite some distance north and is not on a railway line. Her sketched route map heads south from Buta to Lubero on the western bank of Lake Edward. It is not certain which town Theresa meant, but Kasese, the border town north of Lake Edward, in the foothills of Mt. Ruwenzori is the only railway town in this area. BMJ*

The European colonist kindly let us go through and spent some time telling us about the elephant grass covering the slopes and the Bakonjo people, who grew bananas. Near the gold mine, in beautiful country, there was an awful shanty town. Native squatters, whose villages were too far away from work, and without any means of transport, lived in shacks put together from scraps of wood, cardboard and discarded material. We often slowed to have a good look at their living conditions, but the security guard beckoned us on.

Climbing again to the Kabasha Plateau, I slowed the pace up and came to a standstill. "Now what's the matter?", Blenk moaned. "Nothing," I said, then asked her, "Where is the equator?".

King Neptune

Until the advent of long-distance air flights, travellers crossed the equator by ship and the Captain knew from his navigator exactly when and where the ship would cross 'The Line'. A passenger on board crossing the equator for the first time was called a 'Pollywog' - a tadpole not yet a frog, and was about to become a 'Shellback', or veteran sailor. According to Roman mythology, Neptune was the God of the Sea and lived amid the waves. He watched over ships and sailors and His Spirit ruled 'The Deep'. King Neptune was invited aboard by the Captain to perform a nautical ceremony on a Pollywog crossing the Line for the first time.

Anyway, we did not know our exact location nor see any indication of zero latitude. I got off the motorcycle and scratched a line across the gravel-stone track with a stick to mark the equator, the exact bearing being irrelevant for our purpose, but a geographical signpost would have certified it. With the blessing of King Neptune far away in the Indian Ocean, I trumped up the ceremony. As King Neptune, I wanted Blenk to stand up-side-down on the line while I took her picture. Likewise Blenk, as King Neptune, took my picture standing upside down on our mock equator. Natives who came by were puzzled to see barbarian white people doing this tomfoolery in the middle of the track. When we finished this nonsense, we were at the next moment, fully fledged 'Shellbacks' on the other side of the world.

Handstands at the equator!

Kikuyu tribesman with elongated earlobes

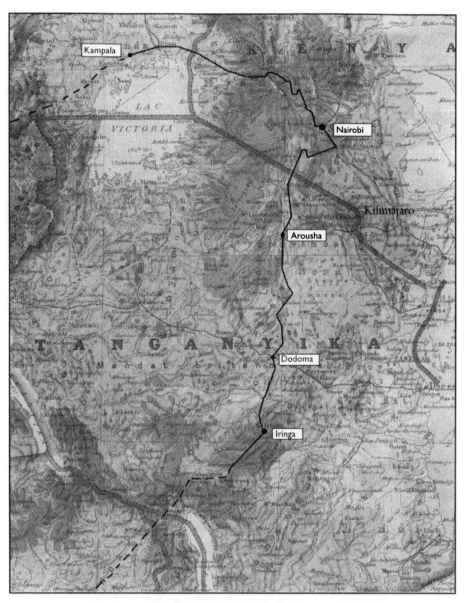

South from Nairobi towards Bulawayo. Dotted line shows uncertain route.

Darkest Africa
Mt Kuwenzori To Nairobi

Having now definitely crossed the equator, somewhere, regardless whether over the mock up line or the true latitude, it did wonders for our moral.

If another vehicle had come along the Kabasha Plateau, there was now at least room to pass, but down from the plateau, the gravel surface came to an end and once again we came across the wide ruts made by motor vehicles.

Near the equator, there are no seasons as dawn, dusk and climatic conditions which depend on latitude, are the same from one week to the next. Though it was now May, we were heading into another winter, this time in the southern hemisphere. At our slow pace in these deep ruts, we did not expect to reach a community for several days and nothing on the map showed anything near here, but the next morning, soon after daybreak, we came to a signpost facing towards us. When we got close enough to read it the sign, written in French and English said: 'TSETSY FLY BELT ENDS HERE'. Unknowingly we had come through a danger zone and had not put up the mosquito net at night.

On the way eastward through mountainous country, crossing the equator in a south-north-south zigzag, we may well have had one wheel in each hemisphere at the same time. Lubero was the first place since Algiers that had a mechanical fuel pump where we did not have to refuel our two-gallon cans poured from twenty-litre containers.

In the rainy season the track was soft and muddy, but new roads were being built, although Congo had yet to have a well defined map. At the Motundu Mission post, we said 'Hello'. I'll never forget their hospitality. Here were English evangelists. This helped our language drawback and they told us much in a short time. Missionaries were the first outsiders to make their way into the interior of Africa. In addition to preaching Christianity, they had introduced education, knowledge of hygiene and agricultural skills. Watussi natives were working on a small cultivated patch nearby, called *shambas*. Watussi people of the Congo and southern Rwanda are a remarkable size, about seven feet tall, and in recent times they have gained recognition in the world of sport and motion pictures of Africa. In contrast the Pygmies of the Congo are the smallest people on earth.

Gorillas

During our short visit we went into a hall where about twenty women were housed. They slept in a double row of cots where there were open fires which were far from hygienic, for cooking snake, crocodile or monkey meat which they liked to eat. Smell and smoke prevented us being in there more than a few minutes, so they all came outside, enthusiastic to meet white women wearing helmets, who looked very strange in travel-stained clothes on a motorcycle that sounded like a rattle-snake. In the medical ward we saw small children with bush sores, infected eyes and sickness in other ways. A native was brought in who, they said, had been mauled by a gorilla, but was suspected of poaching and got himself into trouble, or perhaps here in the mountain home of the gorilla, some ape was looting his cultivated plot of ground for tasty young shoots. In our developed world we seem to loose some of the congeniality we found among the 'uncultured' people in their simple way.

In the Ruwenzori Mountains between Congo and Uganda, a family of gorillas came very close to us and let their presence be known whilst stretching their curiosity. Quite by chance we encountered them, whereas expert trekkers in search of the elusive mountain gorilla, could not have led us to see them any better. As we were riding through a ravine, two of these great apes, one after the other, pounced on the track in front of us by one powerful jump with enough impetus to leap across from one steep slope to high up the incline on the other side. They looked very strong and one of them, if standing upright, might have been five feet tall. They were probably roaming in gentle mood and were inoffensive, provided they were not unduly provoked. We waited for others in the group to pass, once again giving wildlife the right of way, but they took too long and slowly we rolled on, not knowing what the others were up to.

Onward... around the sides of green mountains on twists and turns to ease the gradient, a good road went to the Congo border. All around us we could see bends ahead, behind and below, making it hard to distinguish which we had travelled on from those ahead. We went a very long way to go only a short distance, but the view was worth it.

At 10,000ft, equatorial Africa was cold and wet. A shower came over followed by a downpour of rain which softened the road. Our feet slipped as we pushed in the mud and we were sprayed by the rear wheel with slush that stuck to everything, unlike the desert sand that dropped off. Sunshine followed and soon dried us. The strain of the climb through the mountains broke the rear chain. The rear wheel had to come out to replace the worn sprocket for the new chain, but fiddling with a rivet extractor to make the chain the right length, meant only being able to set chain tension and brake adjustment in the remaining daylight, the rest had to be done in the morning.

Geysers

Next day we saw a mist coming off the ground; in this part of Congo it is like steam rising into the air. To find out what it was, we walked to look over the ridge and saw a strange geological phenomenon of thermal springs coming from out of the ground. Mountains were formed from lava and ash thrown up from openings in the earth's surface, like pressure valves, from which molten rock, fire and steam were - and still are - being discharged.

"Suppose we stay a while", I suggested, "and make the most of all this hot water going to waste?" Blenk agreed we could wash off some of the mud and at the same time, do a little laundry. Over a bubbling hot pool she held a shirt on the end of a stick and seeing how high hot water kept popping up said, sounding like a geologist, "I think this one is a geyser and if it spurts up with more force, I'll loose my shirt!". Our clothes were cleaner, but now yellowish - it did nothing to improve our appearance. They dried enough in the sun, while we made a cup of tea, to repack into the trailer. In such a beautiful country, we decided to camp ... and sleep.

The Ruwenzori mountain range, 'Mountains of the Moon', the small Belgian colony of Ruanda-Urindi and the rough and sometimes stormy water of Lake Edward, some twenty miles wide and a hundred miles long, separate The Belgian Congo from Uganda. Since the days of ancient Egypt the true source of the River Nile had never been certain. Near Khartoum, the capital of Sudan, more than a thousand miles north, two rivers come together to form the Nile proper, flowing through Egypt on its way to the Mediterranean sea, making the River Nile almost the longest river in the world. The source of one river, the Blue Nile, was known to have come from mountains in Ethiopia, and the source of this other river, the White Nile, was believed to originate somewhere here in the southern hemisphere. Two years after we came through here on our motorcycle expedition, mapping of this land was still incomplete. In 1957, a German explorer, Dr Berkhurt Waldecker, discovered the source of the White Nile where the melting snow from the Ruwenzori mountains fed water into the river and into Africa's great lakes.

Dark red garnets were scattered over the ground, and we stopped to collect some of these semi-precious stones. Throughout the ages wearing a gem has had mystical significance and symbolically the garnet was supposed to ward off accidents while travelling.

Uganda

At Kabale in the British Colony of Uganda, was a typical English white painted five-bar gate across the road, exactly like the one that I, as a child, used to crawl through to get to the stables on the other side. But this time well dressed native police, wearing red fezzes and well laundered khaki shorts, opened the barrier for us to enter yet another territory. We now rode on the 'other', left hand, side of the road.

Today was a Sunday. It was the only day of the week when only Ugandan currency was handled and an additional border crossing fee was imposed together with an extra charge for the Uganda passport-stamp. Officialdom being so deeply ingrained, in no way could we get an off duty officer out on a Sunday to exchange francs for pounds-sterling for us to continue, but a staunch British policeman on duty, offered to pay the small amount with his own Ugandan coins of the realm to enable us to get to the capital at Kampala, about four hundred miles away, where we would then pay it back into his bank account. In this incident we were pleased to accept sheer altruism, as it used to be, in the 'good old days'.

On the Ugandan side of the Mountains of the Moon that night, along a stony road and when rounding a bend, an amazing site appeared, the crater of a flaming volcano holding a ball of red fire high in the dark night sky; to witness volcanic activity so clearly was another unusual experience for us; a truly spooky sight.

We travelled through uninhabited woodland country and through a rain shower, wearing cottons that did not soak up much wetness and dried in no time. On the way to Masaka, too tired to ride further, we crawled onto the trailer and slept by the wayside. In the morning, at another Mission station not far away, Blenk knocked at the door expecting to say "Hello" and meet English folk in this British colony. While I waited under their garden bell-tent, the rain came pouring down - just like it did in England. She kept knocking ... it was our luck that a special church service was in progress!

Further along, a truck was sheltering under a tree by the track. We stopped, as is customary, to see if someone needed help. An Indian fellow on his way to Fort Portal had a flat tyre, put on the spare wheel and was now making himself a snack by camp fire under a makeshift rain cover. We introduced ourselves. As we were also chilly, wet and hungry, we unpacked some of our food to share with him and have a good cup of tea. He was interesting to listen to, and told us about how the new railway between Kampala and the Port of Mombasa in Kenya, had opened business for cotton growers and merchants like himself. We left him there and went on to Masaka.

Masaka was a small place with a wide main road, brick houses and shops. Our approach attracted the attention of a resident who stepped from his old car and inquired how far we had come and from where. He was a Dutchman who owned a tea plantation and kindly suggested we follow him as he led the way to the farmhouse making us welcome to stay for the night under shelter from the rain. The plantation was along two miles of rutted side-tracks and the house, atop a short, steep gradient was such that we were almost unable to ride the motorcycle unassisted until tea pickers were beckoned to come and pushed us up the slope.

A crop worker assigned to help us, spread out our sleeping bags and heavy coats to dry in morning sunshine, so that we could pack everything neat and tidy back in the trailer. Besides, some trailer repairs were necessary before we were ready to go on. Incidentally, we had a good home-grown cup o'tea! The Dutchman asked us to stay another day; we were pleased to do so. Since we were already long overdue in Cape Town, having intended to be there a month ago, another day would not make any difference. To have arrived in Cape Town as planned would have meant we hadn't truly 'travelled', since travelling to us was the time spent in different places such as another day here, rather than riding tightly to schedule.

Tea shrubs covered the hillside and rain was good for the plantation. Bantu natives were arranging young plants from seedlings to be planted in well prepared tea fields, while others were weeding and pruning, keeping them pruned down to about five feet. Pruning went on continuously in between pickings. The greyish-green leaves on the branches grew to five inches long, but it was only the new shoots, near the blossoms, that were picked by hand. At sunset the tea pickers went home to their villages.

Tom-toms

Although tired and ready for a good sleep tonight, our host thought we would enjoy a tom-tom party. We heard a drum. Plantation workers from their huts responded to the call. Soon, about twenty men and women from a local tribe gathered with their drums to dance on the lawn behind the house, adapting to the drum-beat, expressing themselves with unrestrained emotion by gestures of sight and sound. It was for us, hard to comprehend. Each hand-hollowed wooden drum gave a different sound. An irregular thump by a lively drummer produced a deep penetrating tone from the very long drum known as 'the African telephone'. Each crop picker was inspired by the tempo. I imagined the old tom-tom in my childhood home, having been silenced for so long, coming alive here and joining the beat.

The drumming continued through the night and by morning a few exhausted souls lay where they dropped on the grass, fast asleep.

Finally, our warm hearted farewell came and as we descended down the steep incline, helping hands kept the laden trailer under control. By noon we had gone, having added another episode to our collection of everlasting memories.

At Mitalamite, less than a hundred miles from Kampala, a company of Indian merchants who were growing cotton, allowed us a safe place to camp. Although lion or leopard were unlikely to be around, there is no knowing where they may roam at night. The ginning-mill was near the cotton fields and before dark we were shown hand-picked cotton being tossed into rollers to separate seed, dust and dirt from fluffy cotton before being pressed into huge bales, stacked ready for shipping. We thanked the Indian owner for our camping site and for allowing us to see the process by which our own clothes were made.

Kampala

At Kampala, native policemen were smartly attired in white topee helmets. They stood on elevated platforms controlling the light traffic, which including an occasional rickshaw. Alongside the wide main wide road of reddish earth, were houses and gardens. We had not seen anywhere since Algiers that was so orderly and regulated. Now in the business district, my first impression was that we had arrived in India because there were so many Indian people here.

The well-established civilian Police organisation did not in any way make the British Colony a 'Police state'. They had an efficient and comprehensive method to administer the Colony. A phone call to the appropriate Department of Information was put through to the Ministry of Internal Affairs and then relayed on until it reached the Chief of Police, who was the rightful authority for our entry into the territory. Of course, now we could speak the same language. The Chief of Police, Captain 'R', swung out of his chair and called to an officer, "What shall we do with these ladies?". The room now bustled with men of the elite uniformed Police corps, sun tanned and regimentally disciplined.

"Sir!," said Officer 'F', "They can have my house", he offered through loyalty and dedication and continued, "I am going on safari and will stay with my colleague tonight". We stayed a week in Kampala in a two-story house, just a short walk from the Embassy with a room each to ourselves. If we had any time to spare, there were jigsaw puzzles and books to read. Our first duty was to go to the bank to pay our debt into the account of the policeman in Kabale who loaned his local currency, bless him, which had allowed us to get here. The bank clerk determined the rate-of-exchange for all our surplus currency and coins that we had accumulated since Agadez. We also got money for Kenya, the next colony en route. These days, credit card holders have a somewhat different way of travelling.

All that was known about Uganda extended back no further than the mid-nineteenth century. Efforts to develop the colony had mostly been done by missionaries. The railway through Kampala had only been built four years earlier during the depression years of the late 1920s, connecting Kampala with Nairobi, in Kenya and the seaport at Mombassa on the Indian Ocean. In the past, commercial trade amounted to killing elephants for the export of ivory and transporting slaves; it now was able to export cotton and coffee. Until the advent of long-distance commercial aircraft, travelling to Uganda, Kenya or other British colonies on the way to South Africa, people had to travel through Egypt and then by boat up the Nile River.

It was here, in Kampala, that our route would link up with the better known Cape-to-Cairo route which, for us at long last, was the end of the unknown, like a light at the end of an African tunnel, from which we had emerged. Uganda and Kenya lay astride the equator which more or less bisected the continent. Algiers was at a latitude of 35.51° North, while Cape Town was 33.48° South, so we had positively done the biggest half of our journey.

The British Empire had established and administered law and justice, through its civilian Police in Uganda, while immigrants from British colonial India had came to Uganda from across the Indian Ocean for commercial opportunities. By dint of their education and financial solvency, they monopolised the plantations and industry and started businesses of their own. The primitive black majority, to whom the previously inaccessible land rightfully belonged, were exploited as cheap labour.

For a while, this tripartite complexity worked well on the surface; life was calm. Shops and businesses closed at the end of a colonial working day and people went home. After closing hours there was nowhere to go. One evening, several off-duty personnel came over to the house where we were staying, to take us for a drive to nearby Lake Victoria where, from the grassy edge of the water we could see alligators. Ripples of water rolled over their glassy eyes and with glittering wet backs, they were ready to plunge out of danger or come towards us - we were ready to run, but they did not move. There were six of us and soon, someone with a 'Limey' twang moaned, "Hey - I'm hungry!" And so too were all of us. As he knew how the civil service functioned, he suggested, "we'll go to the Embassy". The night guard called the Duty Officer; who called the cook; who sent for the servants. House-boys laid out the long dining table, in the main reception hall, with china, glass and silver cutlery, turning strict formality into comedy. The Chief of Police, Captain 'H', was awakened by his batman at midnight. "Sir!," he was told, "dinner is served!". Off-duty 'bobbies' dressed in ludicrous mufti, were also aroused and came to join the nocturnal goings-on.

My thoughts turned back to when I used to work in a factory from morning to night, wearisome and confined, resolving that one day I would seek a different kind of life, but never imagined anything quite so bizarre as this spontaneous midnight dinner party.

Our motorcycle had been cleaned and serviced, courtesy of an auto company. A ladies' hairdresser offered to shampoo and trim our hair, considerably improving our appearance; it felt divine. On May 22nd, 1935, we left Kampala for the Kenyan border keeping an eye open for breaks in the weather from the many showers. We rode out of Uganda with pleasant memories, giving our thanks to good friends with best wishes for a prosperous future. Quite a long way before we reached the next town of Jinja, we found a seemingly unnecessary sign which read, 'Speed limit 20 mph' - it stood on a desolate road. When near to the town, we asked a wayside crop worker - one of about forty tribal groups in the region about it. He told us, "drivers from tobacco plantations come out of side tracks and don't have brakes good enough to stop!".

Kenya

On the Uganda-Kenya border, at the village of Busia, passage from one British colony to another was no more fuss than going from one room to another in the same house. Native border patrols were housed in thatched huts near the workshop and post office hut, but there was no traveller's shelter. It was raining and getting dark, so the guard said it would be alright for us to shelter in the postal annex. That night, safe and comfortable, we had overslept - people waiting the next morning wanted to know why the post office was not yet open!

The road to Nairobi was through open country. It was a good road, but the climb up to the Kikuya Plateau had hillocks that caused us to stall on the steep inclines. We had to inch our way up by means of a rock to wedge the rear wheel, preventing us from rolling backwards, as we had done in so many other places before.

The Young Women's Christian Association (YMCA) hostel in Nairobi was on the outskirts of town and had only just been built. It was set back in grounds which had yet to be landscaped. Reservations for us had been made by the police in Kampala, who had told us about this new branch. We arrived at the entrance of this select two-storey, barrack-like place, looking like a pair of sun tanned rag-a-muffins, wearing torn and stained clothes. We were quite an eye opener to the receptionist who, nevertheless, was expecting us. Then it occurred to her, we were the two young ladies who were riding a motorcycle. Accommodation at the hostel was good and clean which remains a policy of theirs the world over. Upstairs we were given a room each, with soap and towel. These partitioned rooms were tiny and the bed took up most of the space. It included a small dresser and chair. Drops of rain falling on the window outside made us feel we would have a very comfortable night.

However, the hostel seemed strangely empty. Why was it requisite to have made reservation and then find we have the place to ourselves? Apparently, fashionable lady residents had seen us outside, wearing trousers and with a motorcycle. They had put two-and-two together and come to a wrong conclusion; so they were keeping safely out of our way! The front page on the next edition of *The East African Standard* newspaper threw light on the mystery with news of our arrival in Kenya. The headline read, 'CONSTERNATION at The Y.W.C.A!'. Everyone then came around to hear our adventure stories with a thought that, one day, there would be a trans-African highway.

While we repaired the Panther, the only way to get around town, from this outlying location, without a bicycle, was by rickshaw. We hired two Chinese-looking sedan chairs pulled by porters, to take us to the post office and shops or sent them on errands to get us ready to ride through Kenya to Tanganyika.

As much as possible was done to improve the condition of the motorcycle, but wear and tear had made it more difficult to handle. Extreme temperatures made the heat treated coil springs and hair-pin springs lose their tension. Foot gear-change and kick-starter springs were now reinforced with rubber bands cut from an old inner tube. It was a hit and miss affair when we stalled in an awkward place! Saddle springs, if not broken, made the seat feel like sitting on dough while control cables were kinked and gritty, making them stiff to operate. Riding in deep ruts had forced the front forks, steering and sidecar out of alignment and at night we still only had the dim light from our pilot lamp. Nevertheless, I had grown affectionately fond of our faithful 'Dobbin', as if a dear fretting friend, for we still had more than three thousand miles of life together.

Drums at the Uganda tea plantation. Blenk (left) and Theresa

The Southern Hemisphere
Nairobi To Bulawayo

Beyond Nairobi, the capital of Kenya, a sandy road led us through the foothills of Mount Kenya. Although near the equator, it was covered with snow. Then we plunged into wild country. "Look!", I called out, "Zebra!". With their black and white markings, while standing in the shade of trees, they were almost invisible. These were the first zebra outside of captivity that we had seen and was one of the few places where they are to be found. The lion is its main enemy, which meant we were now in lion country. The route dropped down to a lower altitude across open plains, free from mosquito or tsetse fly and, for a while, free from mechanical trouble.

Kikuyu natives were cultivating the soil with hoe and hand tools. Walking towards us was a woman with her companions. She wore a necklace so wide that with each graceful footstep the flat disc of wired beads would swing from side to side. Her companions adorned their ankles with bracelets of ivory and pierced their earlobes with dangling pieces of carved bone, decorated with charms of shiny metal, which was meant to catch the eye. The weight of ornaments stretched the earlobes so they reached down to the shoulders.

The next surprise was to see our first giraffe outside of captivity, trotting over the ground at quite close range, seemingly content while it showed its pace and grace. The giraffe is the tallest of the animal kingdom, yet its long neck has the same number of vertebrae as we have in ours!

On the Athi Plain, a lone rhinoceros had its head down chewing grass, far enough away from the road as not to be disturbed by our motorcycle. We hoped it would go on chewing, but if it happened to look up and come charging towards us with its massive body and short legs, we at least had a head-start. This unwieldy animal can not turn double quick and if it got too close, we could move to one side and let it go by. How many people, I wondered, have seen a really natural rhinoceros? Wildlife in captivity lose some of their lustre and the big game we saw in their natural environment looked more beautiful and majestic than those in the zoo.

As we crossed the tranquil Kenya Plain, we came to railway lines leading to Athi Junction. The daily train had long since departed from the little station, but the waiting-room made a restful shelter for the night, though it turned out not to be so restful! Powerful steam engines in the rail yard were being prepared to replace those arriving on long-distance haul of passengers and freight between

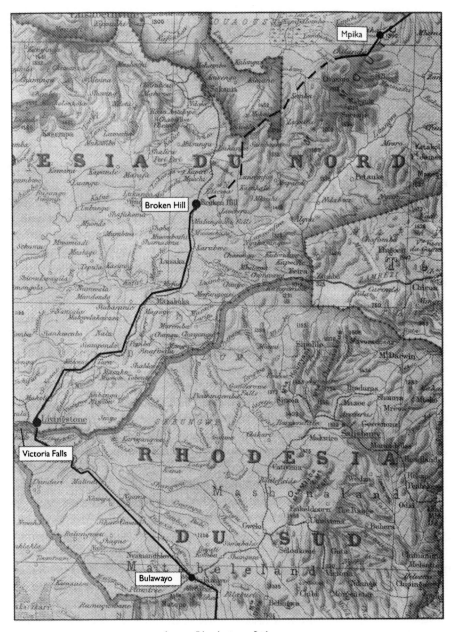

Across Rhodesia to Buluwayo

Cape Town and Kampala and all night long bunkers and boilers were being refilled, while engines shunted back-and-forth to their sidings, crashing into their bumpers! Shrill steam whistles make an awful noise while puffing black smoke over the pristine countryside.

Tanganyika

On 5th June, six months on the trail, we crossed the open border near Arusha where the two British colonies of Kenya and Tanganyika met. We stopped to register our entry into yet another territory. Blenk took the briefcase and passports and walked across the grass between the trees to a residential looking building, while I stayed to protect our belongings from a tormenting pack of monkeys lest one of them would pick up something and take it up a tree.

The name Mount Kilimanjaro, (19,340 ft) means Great Mountain. It was painted on the sidecar so far only as a name but now literally showed its real face, one of the highlights of our journey. We saw for the first time the highest mountain in Africa, so close to the equator, yet capped with snow and set against the blue sky. Of its two peaks, Kilimanjaro (or Kibo) was the highest with Mount Meru, in its foothills, is only 14,500 ft. The next highest in the range was Mount Kenya (16,640 ft), north of Nairobi. They formed a chain of volcanoes through this glorious country.

Slowly we made our way through Tanganyika, the dirt road descended to lower altitude and was flanked by tall brown sun dried grass. Suddenly the motorcycle disturbed something quite close to us; it rustled the grass and we were surprised when two lions, gentle as lambs, slowly moved away; hopefully having had their kill for the day.

We cast our eyes on either side of us along the ground and across the plain on the lookout for movement of wildlife under cover of tall grass, hoping the sound of our motorcycle would warn any creature lurking nearby so they would move away not to be startled into attacking us.

These were better days for more than a hundred or so Bantu speaking tribes. Not so long ago they were unmercifully taken to ships waiting on the Indian Ocean coast by slave traders who had made their way into central and southern villages, leaving them thinly populated. We didn't see any of the wayside thatched huts between the wildly spaced towns of white settlers as we had elsewhere. Survivors of the slave trade toiled on the land sustaining themselves, for industry had not yet gained a foothold in Tanganyika.

As we rode south through Tanganyika, it occurred to us that only about sixty years before we came through here, the explorer Henry Morton Stanley had found the missionary, Dr David Livingstone in the wilds. It seemed nothing much since then had changed - it was still a rough ride!

Influenced by the work of early missionaries in German South West Africa (now Namibia), Germany had been encouraged to construct a railroad from the capital at Dar es Salaam on the Indian Ocean. They were interested in their own colonial expansion and as recently as 1912, many Germans settled here with a genuine desire to build roads and develop the territory as their German East Africa. They had diligently established a road maintenance plan, under a Public

Works Department, with a road construction depot every ten miles across Tanganyika. Each depot was numbered in sequence; PWD 7 meant that we had come seventy miles. However, on the outcome of World War l, Germany lost her African Empire in 1918. During the great depression between the two wars, there was concern about Hitler wanting return of the colony and the German influence never left these people and their penetration into the wilderness continued. Cutting its way through land cleared for an earth road through the mountains to lower altitude, we followed the route to Dodoma.

Melting snow, trickling down the mountain slopes, flowed over the track in places, making a muddy ditch deep enough to get stuck. The PWD had made paved channels, called 'drifts' for the water to flow across the track. These were not too deep for our wheels to go through, but they were also good watering places for wildlife. One night our headlight reflected an eye at a drift and fearing wildlife, I stopped and waited for it to move. Blenk spoke up, "what are you waiting for?". Pointing to it with a quiet voice, I replied "I'm waiting for it to move." She yelled back at me, "that thing won't move - it's a PWD drift reflector!"

Each side of us was over-grown, with nowhere to get off the dirt road to camp. I don't know who thought of the idea to stop at PWD 10. Nobody was there. Blenk looked over the stack of signs and picked out 'KEEP LEFT'. "Will this do?", she asked, then she held out some other signs: 'CAUTION', 'ROAD WORKS', 'KEEP RIGHT' and putting these all around us, we slept in the roadway. We were not disturbed and heard nothing go by!

Our first accident

One afternoon, in the foothills of the Singida Mountains, about four hundred miles into Tanganyika, we were unfortunately struck in the side by the only car we had seen. It had come northbound, around one of the many blind turns. The impact broke the car's steering king-pin and knocked off their left side front wheel. Their car plunged its nose to the ground. It also broke our sidecar suspension so that our front now also scraped the ground. Luckily, no one was hurt. The car had an Indian merchant representing a Ugandan cotton company. He and his porters were going to his office in Kampala before returning to India.

The good-natured gentleman was very, very apologetic. Indeed, we were sorry for the damage done to each other. His car could not move at all and our own ability to carry on was made very difficult. The effect the accident had on the Indian gentleman, finding himself in this predicament, was one of utter helplessness and we realised that in a situation like this, not even money was any help. Confronted with the prospect of spending the night by the wayside, he took solace from the fact that it was quite usual for us to be doing this, even in a tsetse-fly zone, that he must also wait under the stars until sunrise. In time another vehicle would cone along.

The porters made a fire and cooked our rice and made tea. "Nobody will come tomorrow," grumbled a porter adding, "it's Sunday." Blenk, thinking out loud said "today is Wednesday!", but the Indian gentleman told us it was Thursday and nobody could be sure which day of the week it was. I thought to myself "does it matter?"

Taganyika: the damaged car

In the morning someone travelling northward did happen to come along. He was able to take them to Arusha. We floundered along the Masia Steppe with our damaged sidecar, taking turns to stand on the trailer hitch behind, to raise the front of the sidecar off the ground. We did this for about fifty miles, all the way to Dodoma. The Indian gentleman's wrecked car was unable to be moved and remained partly blocking the road. This gentleman later wrote to us from his home in Bombay. The letter was in admiration of our expedition and our philosophical frame of mind on that night of the accident. It contained a cheque for a small sum of money, as a token of friendship with a suggestion that our book be called "*The Rugged Road of Africa*".

In the wide open country on the way to Dodoma, we came across an official two-man inspection team. They had butterfly nets with which to inspect every inch of our equipment, outside and inside the trailer, looking for any trace of the deadly tsetse fly. We also had to ride through a shallow trough of arsenic solution to decontaminate our tyres and wheel rims. They explained that the inspection, to a small extent, was a start of a programme to control the spread of sleeping-sickness over enormous areas of Africa. This was part of a co-operative effort by natives, cattlemen and the government, all doing the best they knew how to prevent a single concealed insect being carried to another region. Today, more scientific methods and aerial insecticide spraying are used. I forgot to ask if they ever caught one! It seemed to me just as futile to catch a fly in Tanganyika as it took to find the proverbial needle in a haystack.

A Bantu mechanic from one of the hundred and twenty so different tribes around Dodoma, made a crude pair of metal brackets to repair the sidecar and support the front springs. We were once again fully functional after the collision with the Indian gentleman. We went on to Iringa, a good two hundred mile ride out of the hills onto the Plain of Iringa. We were able to made up some of our slow progress of the last two days.

The Aga Khan

At Iringa, Asian Indians were preparing for a Moslem celebration. The occasion was the mutual birthdays of lman-e-Faman, the Right Honourable, His

Highness Sir Sultan Mahomed Shah Agakhan P.C, G.C.V.C etc, with his beloved sons Prince Aly S Khan and Prince Sadrudeen. Our arrival at Iringa prompted the host to extend an invitation to us as their guests of honour. At first we were hesitant to accept the kind invitation, as never before had our way worn appearance been more poignantly felt. To attend looking travel-stained and quite unsuitably dressed, we felt would be disrespectful amongst the influential people gathered here in their best attire. Instead, we were given a hearty welcome. Tea and refreshments served near the Mosque was a tasty variation from our usual bland fare. On the grass were games for the children. Today was June 11th, a red-letter day for us too, exactly six months into the journey.

The title 'Aga Khan' was given to the spiritual leader of their Nazari Isamaili sect of Shiite Moslems. Hundreds of years ago, the first Aga Khan claimed he was the direct descendant from Ali, son in law of the Prophet Mohammed. The present Prince Aly Khan was descended from him and the later Aga Khan IV, Prince Karim, studied at Harvard University. All had shown worldly as well as spiritual concern throughout the Moslem lands, including this celebration at the Shia Imami Isamaili Jamat, in Tanganyika.

The British Colony of Northern Rhodesia lay on the southern border of Tanganyika, about two hundred miles south of Iringa. On the hilltop nearby, we stood where it was possible to see into three separate colonies: Looking straight ahead, due south, was Northern Rhodesia where the land of Cecil Rhodes had not yet changed. To the east we looked into the British colony of Nyassaland and turning about to return, we looked out over Tanganyika.

Rhodesia

"RHODESIA," said the border officer in broken English, for it sounded like, "Road Easier", but was not what he meant! Sand carried in the wind, much like Sahara sand, knows no bounds and sand was being blown northward from the Kalahari Desert and drifted with the wind further and further away, covering the track here with reddish dust which gave name to this route as the 'Red Route to the Cape".

Here in Northern Rhodesia, as in its seven neighbouring colonies along it's borders, we passed clusters of thatched round huts and Bantu tribes, some of whom may not have been there very long. After a while, the land close to a village deteriorates and they move to a new place, or perhaps, an army of driver ants drives them out. Driver ants are feared by natives and wildlife alike; even elephants are afraid of them. These ferocious ants ravage everything in their path, stripping the flesh off those animals unable to find water to swim in and drown the ants. Neither burning nor burying them will block the path of driver ants.

Mechanical problems began to happen one after another. Fifty miles from Mpika the throttle cable broke and had us stuck in the dark at a place with no other name than "lion country". We were unable to replace it until daylight. Flat tyres were too numerous to recall. Inner tubes were already dotted with patches and now, the last of our new ones put on the rear wheel. At another place, the engine refused to start. I wiped off the grubby high tension lead and put in one of our last new spark plugs. We stopped at Mpika to attend to clutch trouble before it got worse. Oil had leaked onto the dry clutch-plates and the clutch was now slipping badly; the clutch springs had lost their tension. We washed out the clutch-plates in petrol and inserted under each clutch-spring, a washer to increase the tension. This probably had something to do with the clutch cable breaking later!

I peeled off a short bit of the outer casing to reveal the broken clutch-cable, and pushed the inner cable into an emergency pinch-bolt, intended for this purpose. Rubber bands cut from old inner tubes held things together, such as the broken battery-case bracket and plenty of these rubber bands were kept stretched behind the license plate. The entire machine was by now held together by nuts and bolts taken from where they could be spared. At one point the front brake anchor-arm came adrift and we lost the nut off the spline! In addition to wire, string and rubber bands we used our initiative - chewing gum was used to seal leaks in the fuel tank and a water container. All but the most serious breakdowns could be taken care of as we continued on our way.

A change of direction

The information we heard at Mpika about road conditions ahead very likely saved us some trouble. A lorry driver told us that his party had taken six days to come north from Salisbury (now Harare), the capital of Southern Rhodesia. For over six hundred miles, there lay deep ruts and elephant grass, fifteen feet high, so on that account we altered our planned course.

The Victoria Falls route to South Africa took us far away from the ruins of Zimbabwe in Southern Rhodesia, that we had hoped to see. These stone age relics date back 500,000 years. Zimbabwe is the revered name of the now independent nation, which was formerly Southern Rhodesia. I wondered about everything we had seen so far. Who indeed was the 'sleeping giant' - China or Africa?

Like driver ants, we kept going. We never had a normal day. We had no radio contact with the outside world, nor music to relieve the monotonous drone of the engine. Each day was a challenge. In the southern hemisphere mid-winter month of June, each night of restful sleep was under a full moon and stars. I never knew the moon could look so big or the stars so bright. Running through the wooded country and grassland, the nearest town was some 300miles away at Broken Hill, Northern Rhodesia. It is now known as Kabwe and lay alongside a railway line. There was a growing mining centre here, and artifacts had been discovered of early inhabitants who lived here 25,000 years ago.

In the small hotel, "The Crested Crane", owned by white settlers who built it, we enjoyed the luxury of clean hot water baths, comfortable beds and although out of the mosquito zone, mesh screened windows. Now we no longer needed our daily dose of quinine against malaria. We worked on the Panther in the courtyard and putting the trailer in order, we prepared to leave in the morning.

Late next afternoon, as lookout passenger in the sidecar, I saw in the distance a trail of rising dust. "Look!" I shouted to draw Blenk's attention from avoiding potholes and steering through sand drifts, "there's something coming." "Something coming?", she repeated - what speed are they doing to make a dust like that - can they see dust at our speed?". In such desolate places, travellers usually stop to meet each other. The dust settled and two white ladies hopped out of their car onto the sandy track making a four-woman gathering in the wilderness.

Miss N. and her sister were driving to Broken Hill and we all asked each other questions quicker than any of them could be answered. The sisters were anxious to reach their destination before dark and curtailed our brief encounter with one regret - that they would not be home to invite us to stay a night, especially when we were so close to where they lived. Miss N. writing a note, smiled and said "give this to my House boy and stay at our house anyway". She described exactly where to go: "In about thirty miles look out for a wooden signpost - be careful not to miss it", she continued to explain in detail " .. it says LUSAKA." With one finger pointing eastward, she told us, "one day, one day, Lusaka will be our new capital."

We saw the wooden signpost at the corner of a sandy side-road which pointed to Lusaka and turned left, as sketched on the piece of paper. At the three bungalows, we stopped by the middle one with its pretty garden. An alert house boy, called the Head-boy, read the letter and went about his loyal duty. We paid for the food that the servants prepared for us and used our own cutlery. We slept on their beds in our own sleeping-bags and had the freedom of the house. We relaxed on the veranda in easy chairs where hand-carved ebony and ivory pieces were arranged that conveyed to us the spirit of our absent hosts, whom we would never see again. May the goodwill of those days never be forgotten. We left a note there to at least say "Thank you" before we departed.

Lusaka now has one of the finest tree-lined boulevards with modern architecture, wide streets and shopping centre and like most capitals, administrative buildings house government and industry. But I will always remember Lusaka from that little wooden signpost at the corner of a sandy lane. The ride of about two hundred miles south to the old capital of Northern Rhodesia, at Livingstone, was the most easily covered mileage since Algiers. Incidental, the least mileage in twelve hours of daylight in the Sahara was twenty-five miles, but now we were keeping the speed down now, as the Panther was almost worn out.

The Victoria Falls

The Victoria Falls are situated about mid-way between east and west coasts, latitude 25.35°S, along the course of the two thousand mile long Zambezi River. It was discovered by Dr David Livingstone and named in honour of Queen Victoria. For many years the Kololo natives had seen from five miles away the spray rising into the air and hearing the terrific roar of the plunging torrent of water, but were afraid to come close to the 'Smoke that Sounds'. The Mayor and Mayoress of Livingstone kindly greeted us on arrival after a day long ride over the red dust road. Nobody under the sun could have been a better escort for us than this spectacle. The grandeur of the Victoria Falls lies in the remarkable way tiny islands, with trees and plants, stand in the way of the flow of water and channel the rushing mile wide waters of the Upper Zambezi River as they flow into gigantic fissures or cracks in the river-bed, to plunge down over the edge of the zig-zag breach and fall into what is known as the 'Boiling Pot', into the Lower Zambezi River, some three hundred and fifty feet below in Southern Rhodesia.

We spent a day all around the falls and saw it again at night. A seldom seen spot was a place where some madcap, by name of Mr Brew, had smoothed off horizontal rocks enough on which to sit, then lower the feet to reach another smoothed off stage to sit, repeating the procedure until the result of his handiwork were a set of steps, known as the Brew Steps. One behind the other, we stepped down without getting too wet from the spray, to see the falls from below. Standing for a few minutes on my step, I listened to the roar of the torrent of water that had scared the natives and looking up awe struck, I perceived the great spectacle as a number of unrelated parts grouped together like a grand finale of a musical suite. I wondered, what if Mendelssohn could have seen and heard the falls as he did the waves breaking against the Scottish coast to compose his "Hebrides Overture"? Or of Grofe, who wrote the "Grand Canyon Suite". Could a composer write a musical impression of the gorges and mini-rapids? These were called the Cataracts; the Knife-edge; Leaping Water; Rainbow Falls - where the spray in sunlight has a permanent rainbow and of Danger Point, as themes where all the waters plunged into the Boiling Pot, into Southern Rhodesia, below. I wondered how a 'Victoria Falls Suite' might sound?

Along the way to Hwange, we met a twelve-pair mule team hauling a wagon of felled trees, making its way through virgin woodland. They travelled alongside the road, which though well-intended, the size of that load still made it difficult for anything to pass. We went slowly by just to watch how he manhandled twenty-four mules. As we rode on, we passed thatched villages of Ndebele and Shona tribes in Matabeleland, quite close together to cultivate the land. In contrast, the colonial settlers in Southern Rhodesia, had built their homes and established private enterprise in towns more than a hundred miles apart.

Bulawayo

With a name like Bulawayo, we had expected to come across another native settlement, but were surprised to find our wheels rolling on a real road. It was a tell-tale approach to a modern town. The smooth wide-paved avenue was like riding in paradise and lead to an industrial centre by a railway. Bulawayo was the first big city since Algiers. Along the main boulevard, the skyscrapers and new shops reflected brilliant sunshine. The elite Carlton Hotel attracted my attention. "We can't go in THERE!" countered Blenk, uneasy about our travel-worn appearance. "Why not?" I replied and explained "this is not New York", but before I made my point, she was tempted to yield to the exorbitance of a warm bath, a good meal and a soft bed. She was inclined to agree that other weary travellers like us went in there, too, but I am sure nobody looked quite so shabby! It didn't take much battery acid to make holes in our clothes.

At Look-Out Point, twenty-five miles south of Bulawayo in the Matopos Hills, we stood on the rocks by the grave of Cecil Rhodes. He left England when he was seventeen years old and went to Africa where he made a fortune having discovered diamonds. He went back to England to study at Oxford University and returned to the colony to become Prime Minister. As a statesman, he extended the railway from Cape Town, through Bulawayo to the Zambezi River, with a vision of a Cape-to-Cairo rail-link. In 1905, a road-and-rail bridge spanned the

Victoria Falls gorge over the Zambezi River. It was of plain yet functional design, that looked to me like a giant coat-hanger up in the air and linked trade routes with Uganda and shipping ports at Mombassa. Cecil Rhodes left most of his fortune for education and many famous people were former Rhodes scholars.

During my school days it was hard for me to sit still and listen to dreary history lessons about missionaries and explorers who left Europe to become Empire builders and find new land, gold and diamonds, making treaties with native Chiefs. But from my first-hand experiences, I came to understand those history and geography lessons, which had at long last, taken on some real meaning for me.

Elated by the fact that in about one-hundred-and-fifty miles, we would cross our last frontier and reach the Union of South Africa, the route now offered nothing else to be excited about. Press reports mentioned our progress and news from the colonial media reached home. Even our worst adversaries of the venture were at long last to witness we had fulfilled our ambition to reach Cape Town. We felt confident and justified in having such high hopes to accomplish what we set out to do.

Blenk and Theresa (right) with damaged chassis springs causing the sidecar to scrape the ground.

The Last Thousand Miles
Bulawayo To Cape Town

The first signpost pointing in the direction of Cape Town stood at a road junction in Beitbridge. Seven months to the day, July 11th, we rode over the bridge, named after Alfred Beit - man-Friday to Cecil Rhodes - and crossed the Limpopo River. We were now in the Union of South Africa. Table Mountain here we come!

The first signpost to Cape Town at Beaufort West - 400 miles to go!

Customs soon cleared our documents at the border town of Messina. The film *Africa Speaks* was being shown in the cinema and we were given complimentary tickets to see the Show. Friendly Dutch settlers invited us to their home for the night and the next day a French lady asked us to lunch. Finally, we set off to Pretoria, two hundred and fifty miles away at the administrative centre of the Union. In the Kruger National Wildlife Reserve, thirty miles south, a game warden stood by the gate of his wayside cottage to interrogate us, as he did all those who go through the reserve. According to regulations, only closed vehicles were admitted, stating that "Travellers must keep windows closed; drivers and passengers stay inside. No hunting, shooting or tossing food to animals." He was

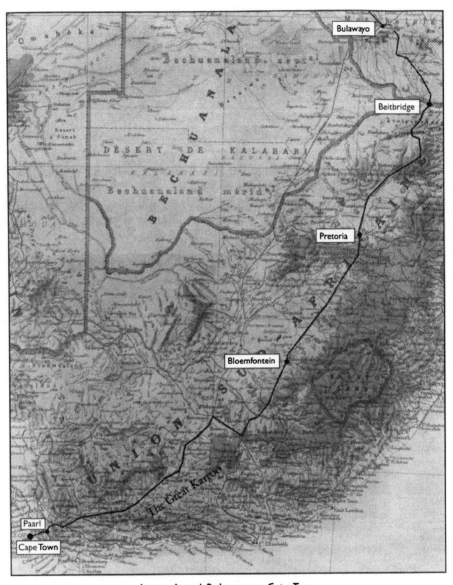

Journey's end: Bulawayo to Cape Town.

baffled by a motorcycle. Already we had been through open country teeming with wildlife, yet here we were expected to abide by these restrictions.

I said "No, we have no fruit or candy". Blenk went on to explain - as if the game warden didn't already know - "besides, elephants have a keen sense of smell and could sniff a car and crush it to get what it wanted," - to which I added "no animal would want any of our food." Blenk, again, "if an elephant or anything tried to attack, we could accelerate and get away fast." As usual we argued with officialdom, until the warden exercised his limited veto over his masterminds and let the motorcycle go on. Actually, we didn't see any animals at all as they usually keep away from the road.

When north of the equator, in the Sahara, we crossed the Tropic of Cancer. Here, in the southern hemisphere in the Pretoria region, we now crossed the Tropic of Capricorn - an imaginary line drawn around the earth, which the ancients called 'Gateways of the Sun'. These are the furthest latitudes north and south which the sun reaches, giving us our seasons. As the earth turns on its axis, it travels faster at the equator than at the Poles, causing strong air currents to rise, that cool in the upper atmosphere. The cold air falls along the Tropic of Cancer and the Tropic of Capricorn and in these lie the Kalahari Desert, west of here, and other deserts around the world.

So far we had covered thirteen thousand miles of rugged road, taken in desert heat and sand; jungle track; steep slippery hills; humid mist; tropical storms; cold high mountains or no road at all. At times we pushed and coaxed the motorcycle along. Now on good road it was still hard to make good speed as our Panther was by now very much the worse for wear and was slipping out of gear from a well worn transmission. At Pietersburg we stopped to see what to do about it and obtained thick car transmission oil to take up the slack - something Burmans, the gearbox manufacturer, would never have recommended - hoping that in the cooler weather, it would not leak through the worn bearings. So, for the remaining journey to Cape Town we restrained our speed to take good care of our P&M Panther and keep it panting to the end of the road.

Pretoria, capital of the Transvaal Province and administrative centre of South Africa, was not such a big place as it is now. But at the thrill of us reaching here, we were given a letter of introduction to General Smuts - Prime Minister of the Union between 1919-24; statesman; soldier and philosopher. It was expected that he would be re-elected in 1938 as Head of State.

Front page headlines in the Transvaal newspapers brought out well-wishers and local motorcycle riders, who escorted us to Polly's Restaurant for a reception. Next morning, by appointment, we were ushered to the executive chambers to be received by General Smuts, who raised himself from behind his desk and shook our hands as we sat down. The General was interested in our venture and asked questions about our experiences, our health and our equipment commenting on the unusual way of coming overland by motorcycle. After many minutes he wished us a pleasant journey through South Africa and signed our autograph books, saying his own idea of a good holiday was a trek through the wilds.

Johannesburg was the industrial capital and largest city in the Union of South Africa and lay some thirty-six miles south. Crowds of black and white South Africans cheered and waved as we made our way along the road approaching the City. Barriers were placed near City Hall to make a passage-way through the enormous crowd for our arrival for a civic reception; it was 2.00pm, Tuesday, 23rd July. Outside City Hall we dismounted from the motorcycle and walked up the stately flight of steps to where the Mayor and Mayoress Mr and Mrs Freeman were standing, looking very dignified with their Chains of Office.

In his speech, The Mayor said, "This is the beginning of an age of record-breaking, whether to fly the fastest, the longest or to ride a motorcycle down the length of Africa, has value."

Gold!

The Witwatersrand Gold Mine invited us to go down the gold mine. In the control room of one of the deepest gold mines in the world, we were briefed on procedure and what to expect about air pressure and angles of descent and were shown the under-ground plan which we would follow, down below. Then we were fitted with helmets, handed our lamps and we signed the indemnity form. At the minehead two guides waited for us as the cage brought up personnel from underground. The clattery iron grilled gate of the small elevator slammed shut with about six of us crammed together inside ready to go down the shaft. Then the cage dropped so suddenly the weight came off my feet.

On the way down, just as explained to us in the office, the speed of the cage slowed. Here it entered the worked-out part of the mine or 'fault' at the end of a gold reef where a natural occurrence in the earth's crust had changed the angle of descent until it reached a place further along where the gold vein was exposed again and mining resumed about 10,000 ft below the surface. In the dim light of our lamps, we could see between the bars of the open-grated cage, the rough wall of the quarry as it flashed by until we slowed and very gently stopped at the landing stage, more than two miles underground. We had to stoop beneath the hefty cross-beams or 'headers' here and there, all the way along the man-made cave, accompanied by very informative guides. Our lamps shed light upon the gold-bearing face of quartz between layers of rocks and except for a break or a fault, the vein extended for hundreds of miles, gradually sloping down deeper and deeper.

Ore, like coal and iron, was dug out of the mine. Gold was then separated from the ore by a complicated refining process and weighed and measured by the 'carat', the unit of weight for gems. Pure gold is 24-carat, but gold is a soft metal and is seldom used in its pure form, so a 12-carat gold piece means it is half gold and half some other metal.

We walked back to the underground landing stage where a cage was waiting to bring us up the long haul to the surface. We returned to the office, not at all that dirty, for it was very clean and cool down there. We handed back the equipment, thanked the staff and our guides for a wonderful experience to add to our bank of golden memories. Then Blenk and I were presented with a surprise souvenir, each of us were given a nugget of quartz containing a glittering lump of gold.

The Vaal River had a good modern bridge to ride over and we left Transvaal Province, and entered the Orange Free State heading for Bloemfontein, the Provincial capital. A gravel road ran through flat grassland country and we had nothing of special interest to see or to occupy the mind for about two hundred and sixty miles. No other vehicle or sign of life human or animal was seen for several days; nor did we converse much.

A time to reflect

I don't know what Blenk was thinking about during this dismal stretch as we gradually approached Cape Town. I had time to think about how much motorcycling meant to me and in the motorcycling fraternity, how I had met another woman, Florence Blenkiron of equal mind. Yet, some people consider a motorcycle to be a mechanical hazard. Certainly riders do fall off, but so too do people on foot, or from a horse or a bicycle, mostly due to a mistake or carelessness. A motorcycle is safe and useful; very economical and enjoyable to own and to believe otherwise is as foolish as to doubt that of a brick wall. One day, I thought to myself, I would have a riding academy and research the technique of motorcycle riding.

"LOOK!", Blenk shouted from the saddle, interrupting my thoughts: "Look at that shanty town". Across the flat prairie land approaching Bloemfontein, we could see a fenced in compound where natives lived who worked in the town, but under the heel of apartheid were not permitted to live there. Yet their *kraals* and families were too far away for them to walk to work every day without transport. For only part of the year were they able to live in their own homes. Meanwhile they lived on the outskirts of a "White man's town", to be near work, living crowded together in shacks crudely put together from cardboard packing material, bits of wood and scraps of sheet metal. These stood side-by-side to support each other in such shameful living conditions, that they had to be seen to be believed.

The last frontier

On July 25th, 1935 we left behind the Orange Free State Province and crossed the last frontier, over the Orange River Bridge into the Cape of Good Hope Province. The last hurdle lay ahead, to ride across the Great Karroo, the barren plateau at an average altitude of 3,000 ft. This was about three hundred miles long and seventy miles wide, where nothing much grows except briefly when it rains. Tufts of growth, covered with dew would become patches of ice in the July winter when it was terribly cold. Riding on stony ground for dreary hours across the Great Karroo, heading toward the distant horizon, the last frayed throttle control cable made it difficult to keep the engine running smoothly. Without meeting a soul or seeing a tree, we kept to our own thoughts.

Soon we would be going home. Again we would be asked, as we had many times already, "Why did you do it?" We would be asked about people and ethnic groups, wildlife, lions, elephants and snakes; of our many adventures and why we broke away from the conventional and lived our own lives?

Along the lonely Karroo, I recalled the scenario of the seven month 14,000 mile journey down the African continent, like an artist who cannot see the sun, tries with dark and light colours to convey sunrise or sunset across a landscape. I would make use of word-paintings to describe places and happenings of our expedition. The dark side would be the shanty towns. The bright side was discovering Africa. Despite the hardship, we had the time of our lives and learned much when wandering around in contact with thought provoking people in interesting places. There were occasions for despair, but with our self-reliance and clear objective we never lost enthusiasm. It was not an easy task, but we gained more worldly wisdom out of it than ever expected. I summed up my impression by saying to myself a few lines from E.A. Guest:

> Somebody said it couldn't be done,
> But he with a chuckle replied,
> That maybe it couldn't, but he would be one
> Who wouldn't say so till he'd tried.
>
> So he buckled right in with a trace of a grin
> On his face - if he worried he hid it.
> He started to sing as he tackled the thing
> That couldn't be done, and he did it.

We reached the end of the Great Karroo and the end of our daydreaming, with a tinge of excitement as we descended to the fertile agricultural country at Beaufort West. The beginning of the end of our adventure would come in about another two hundred miles at the town of Paarl, just outside Cape Town.

The final leg

On 28th July, 1935, we were greeted with open arms by our friends Faye and Bert, at their vineyard. We had been corresponding all the while we were planning the trip. Instead of an English cup of tea, we drank a toast of their good South African wine. The day left just enough time for their Afrikaaner native South African vine gardener, to show us their vines. The vineyards of Paarl, in a fine grape growing region, produce what is considered to be wine of the best quality. He explained that vines from Europe were first planted on the lower slopes of Table Mountain by early Dutch settlers, where the climate was both moist and sunny and the soil contained nutrients to give grapes their special flavour. We saw the large vats where crushed grapes and juice were fermenting naturally, with nothing extra added, before they were placed in wooden casks for longer fermentation. Later in the distillery, the connoisseur of the harvest described to us the distinguishing features of a superior wine, but even so we were inexperienced in the art of wine-tasting and were hardly able to tell one from another.

That night in their home, we talked about former times together in England and the next morning, uneasy about giving us any more of their intoxicating

The end

brew before we rode into Cape Town, they generously packed a case of red wine for us to celebrate on arrival there.

At long last, almost eight months since leaving London, the thrilling sight of the flat-topped Table Mountain, (3,570 ft) the land-mark of Cape Town, came into view. An Atlantic breeze blew over the travel stained and somewhat battered motorcycle which slowly made its way to the southern-most end of the continent. We rode along the main Adderly Street, lined with well-wishers and an escort of international press, to City Hall. The Governor General of the Union of South Africa, Mr and Mrs Gardner, together with a cheering crowd, greeted us in sunshine. The Earl of Clarendon, representing the United Kingdom in this Colony, received us later in his office to celebrate the expedition which had established a new record.

Our safe and happy arrival in Cape Town was the end of a marvellous exploit and we had the satisfaction to know it was the first north-south crossing of the African continent. We were fortunate to have seen Africa the way it was, before politicians made our journey impossible. Our journey was at an end. It was Monday 29th July, 1935.

Epilogue

Tell me thou Vagabond whose Conscience I be,
"Whyfore are you restless and disturbing me?"
Sway me not like a tree blown down by a gale,
To uproot my guardian Conscience, so frail.

Tell me thou Conscience whose vagabond I be,
"Will the challenge of Life not harken to me?"
Deep within our soul that unites us as One,
These questions of many are answered by none.

Theresa Wallach

Editor's notes:
The political map of Africa has changed considerably since Theresa and Florence crossed the vast continent. These changes occurred as the member nations of the British and French Commonwealths sought independence, and in so doing the names of many of the places referred to in Theresa's manuscript have changed. As far as possible, contemporary names have been used throughout. Modern names have been included when necessary.

Most of North West Africa came under French jurisdiction in the late 19th century. The constitution of the Fifth French Republic, promulgated in 1958, envisaged a French Community of states. Though many of the former Colonies have gained full independence they remain closely linked to France.

Algeria, annexed to France in 1862, gained its independence in 1962.

French West Africa, comprising the colonies of Mauritius, French Sudan, Senegal, French Guinea, Ivory Coast, Dahomey and Niger was broken up in the 1950s and 1960s. Niger elected to become an autonomous Republic within the French community, but in 1960 gained full independence. Dahomey also became an independent Republic in the French community in 1958 and gained its independence in 1960. In 1990 it changed its name to the Republic of Benin.

French Equatoria, in the heart of Africa, comprised the colonies of Chad, Ubangui-Chari, Cameroons, Gabon and the Middle Congo. Chad became a member state of the French community in 1958 and gained its independence in 1960. Fort Lamy was renamed N'Djamena and remained its capital while Fort Archambault was renamed Sarh. Ubangui-Chari likewise elected to remain in the French community in 1958 but gained full independence in 1960, changing its name to The Central African Republic.

The Congo was founded in 1885 and became a Belgian colony in 1908. It gained its full independence in 1960. Ruanda-Urindi, administered by the Belgian Congo, suffered internal rebellion between the Hutu and Tutsi peoples and in 1962 gained its independence and became Rwanda.

The British Empire likewise succumbed to calls for independence, but most of its former colonies remain within the Commonwealth. The Federation of Nigeria gained independence as a Member of the Commonwealth in 1960 and became a Republic in 1963. Uganda gained independence in 1962 and became a Republic 1967. Kenya gained independence in December 1963 and became a Republic in 1964.

Tanganyika gained its independence within the Commonwealth in 1961 and became a Republic in 1962. The Zanzibar territory, ruled by the Sultan of Zanzibar under British protectorate gained its independence in December 1963, and in April 1964 united with Tanganyika to form the United Republic of Tanzania.

The former British protectorate of Nyasaland, part of the Federation of Rhodesia and Nyasaland, assumed internal self-government in 1963, gained independence as Malawi in 1964 and became a Republic in 1966. Its neighbour, Northern Rhodesia came under British rule in 1889. When the Federation was dissolved in 1963, it became an independent Republic within the Commonwealth in 1964 as Zambia.

Southern Rhodesia gained self-government in 1923, but made a Unilateral Declaration of Independence in 1965. In 1980 it gained full independence as the Republic of Zimbabwe and remains in the Commonwealth.

The British protectorate of Bechuanaland became the Republic of Botswana in 1966 and remains in the Commonwealth.

The colony of the Cape of Good Hope alternated between Dutch and British rule until 1806. Following many conflicts, the Orange Free States, Natal, Transasvaal, Zululand etc combined as the Union of South Africa in 1910. The Union gained independence within the Commonwealth as early as 1931 and in 1961 became the Republic of South Africa.

Appendix A: The Return Journey
by Barry M Jones

Reports of the adventure were dispatched to *The Daily Sketch*, *The Motor Cycle* and *Motor Cycling* in London at various points along the way. These brief reports make interesting reading when compared to Theresa's *Rugged Road* account; for example in *Motor Cycling* of 29th May 1935, they report: ".. they arrived in Kampala (Uganda) on Wednesday last. They described their journey across the desert as uneventful and the Arabs and others whom they met were very friendly. The girls left for Nairobi the following day."

I wonder what Theresa and Florence actually meant by "an uneventful" desert crossing? In a *Motor Cycling* report carried on 10th July, 1935, they say: "On Wednesday last (3rd July) they arrived at Broken Hill, North Rhodesia after a journey full of incident. Conditions were quite favourable for motorcycling through Kenya and Tanganyika Territory and the girls were able to make up time after their many delays on other parts of the route."

In August 1935, *The Motor Cycle* carried a three page account of the complete journey to Cape Town. It presented a route map which had been prepared before the journey took place, but had not been updated to take into account the diversion which took them to the Victoria Falls rather than the third century ruins at Zimbabwe. For Theresa, the Victoria Falls were a truly natural wonder of the world and when she visited the Niagara Falls in 1946, she found these far less awe inspiring!

The Motor Cycle article went on to remark how the pair intended making a return run to England but were awaiting arrival of a new Panther, registered AWU 771 and to be christened *The Venture II*, which P&M was sending out to them. According to both Theresa and these magazine reports, the original *The Venture* was still in excellent order, so the magazine presumed the new motorcycle was an insurance policy for a safe return. But things were not what they seemed.

Parting of the ways

They arrived at Cape Town on Monday, 29th July 1935 and the intention was that after a month's recuperation, they would return together following the same route. However soon both *The Motor Cycle* and *Motorcycling* were reporting that Theresa was suffering, variously, from a fever or malaria and had been advised by her doctor to make the return journey by sea.

The 9th April 1936 edition of *The Motor Cycle* announced the safe return in London of Florence Blenkiron upon *The Venture II* and they presented a brief account of her return journey. This report inadvertently contained errors, since corrected by Theresa regarding her "return by boat after having the bad luck to fall ill". Theresa insisted to me that she was not medically 'ill' at all but was, in her own words, 'emotionally drained'. It was also reported that Florence had decided to return on her own and "a new outfit was shipped out by the makers (the original outfit had been practically written off in a crash with a car)." Theresa maintained that the original *The Venture* was perfectly roadworthy and wondered if in fact Florence had had a subsequent accident.

The new Panther had a conventional chromed tank unlike the original *Venture* which was fully painted. The new Watsonian sidecar was already painted with the return route and had been christened *Venture II*. It was finished in a deep orange livery.

So what did happen in Cape Town?

Whatever the reason for the ladies splitting up, Florence did try to find a companion in Cape Town for the return journey by Panther combination, but without success. *Motor Cycling* of 25th September advised that Florence had already started her return journey, alone; they later reported she left on 18th September.

The Motor Cycle had yet to catch up with the news and their 3rd October edition advised that Florence hoped to leave at the end of the second week of September! In contrast *Motor Cycling* of 2nd October reported that Theresa has already set sail for home but intended disembarking en route to fly to Nairobi where she would meet up with Florence. *The Motor Cycle* reported on 10th October 1935 that Florence had arrived at Salisbury, Southern Rhodesia and that Theresa had already arrived back in England. Theresa has never mentioned a rendezvous - could it be that her intention was to rejoin Florence to complete the return journey together or did she have second thoughts and continue by sea without stopping? We will probably never know.

Clearly something had badly gone wrong between them. Theresa was certainly the more domineering of the two ladies: to her this was the adventure of a life time, whereas to Florence, it was a means to an end of getting to see family friends in Cape Town. Together, Blenk and Theresa were a good team and had accomplished a fantastic journey, but on reaching Cape Town, Theresa found Blenk's relaxed attitude and lack of exhilaration at having crossed the vast continent dismayed her so much, that she parted company and Theresa became intent on returning to England alone - the impression gained is that she could not see them working together as a dedicated team for what would be a return journey without a cause. This doubtless put Florence in a very tight spot and despite trying to find a companion for the return journey, she was unsuccessful.

Theresa later pointed out that though they had several minor accidents there was none so serious that it couldn't be patched up on the spot, but on one of the many hairpin bends down a mountain road, a car had come around the corner and hit the motorcycle. By Theresa's own account this was not a bad crash and *The Venture* was in a "magnificent", though honourable battle-scarred condition when they reached the Cape! She doesn't know what happened to *The Venture* afterwards; so did perhaps Florence have a subsequent accident in Cape

Town? Theresa always felt *The Venture* should have been returned to England, but it never was and was not even aware that P&M had been asked, possibly by prearrangement, to send out the new motorcycle for Florence's return journey! Clearly, Florence had access to money either from sponsors or through private means and this did upset Theresa, for she had scrimped and saved to make the journey and was now faced with straining her own funds to return to England.

The pair were two quite different people. Theresa found Blenk could be standoffish and unapproachable at times (though in fairness the same has been said by others of Theresa). Indeed Theresa was quite surprised on the day they left London when Blenk pointed to a woman in the crowd and announced that she was her Mother! While Theresa kept a meticulous log book, Blenk never made an entry or recorded her feelings throughout the entire journey. Blenk was also quite tight lipped about business transactions involved in the adventure and in later years this puzzled Theresa, for not one company who afterwards benefited from advertising, approached Theresa for her consent or paid her any royalties. Whatever other deals were struck, such as providing up to date route information to cartographers, it seems these were done by Blenk alone, but then arguably it was she who had completed the return journey and perhaps those business sponsors felt Blenk was the one with whom to deal. However, the impetus of trade advertising following the expedition was soon lost.

The Venture II

Being on her own, Blenk was able to accommodate all her gear in the sidecar and was thus freed from the burden of a heavy trailer. The only mishaps she encountered (or were reported by the press), were broken valve springs, replacement valves, numerous punctures and replacement tyres. The sidecar chassis tube had fractured at one point, which was hardly surprising considering the load she was carrying!

By early October, Florence had reached Salisbury, Southern Rhodesia. From there she travelled to Nairobi staying at a Roman Catholic mission at Faradje and one and a half days at a British Mission school near Niangara. By mid November she arrived in Bula, Belgian Congo. Her route is not recorded in detail but it is evident from her photographs that she went west through the Congo to Nigeria via Marouna in the French Cameroons rather than through Chad and Fort Lamy.

In early January 1936 she arrived in Kano, Nigeria. Until this point, the roads had been of reasonable standard and had presented few problems on their southbound journey. Florence was intent on crossing the difficult Sahara desert alone by following the regular route across the desert used by the SATT vehicles. Wisely, the authorities at Kano were adamant she would not cross the Hoggar Massif and soft sands of the Sahara Desert alone without a substantial guarantee to cover the expenses incurred in a desert rescue. Florence was thus faced with an impossible dilemma; she could wait for another vehicle which might graciously accompany her across the desert or she could admit honourable defeat and take the desert bus to Algiers. After a weeks delay, she decided to effectively end the journey at Kano and allow the Panther combination to be towed on a trailer behind the desert bus. She arrived some three weeks later in Algiers on Monday, 10th February 1936.

By April 1936, Florence had completed her journey by Panther at Rhodesia House in the Strand, and presented a letter from the Prime Minister of South Africa to the High Commissioner for Southern Rhodesia. What occurred during the month of March is not known - did she perhaps enjoy a well earned rest in France?! *Venture II* was then exhibited at the famous Oxford Street, London stores of Selfridges for their 'Sports Week' commencing 4th May, but it was not until February 1937 that Florence presented a detailed lecture to a packed audience of the International Motorcyclist Touring Club at the Cripplegate Institute, London. It was a fabulous expedition which set the hearts of adventurers pounding. Unfortunately her account has yet to be unearthed!

The African adventure demonstrated the tremendous strength and reliability of P&M's Panther Redwing 600cc single and of Watsonian's sidecars - the Panther had already entered the annals of motorcycling history as one of the finest of all sidecar motorcycles. Phelon & Moore and the many other sponsors such as Smiths, Prices Oil ('Motorine B' deluxe engine oil), Lodge spark plugs and Terry's springs, made good use of the publicity surrounding the adventure. Indeed in promoting the 1936 model range, both P&M and George Clarke took out a joint advertisement exploiting this to the full:

"The French military 'plane swoops low to examine the speck crawling slowly on through the illimitable burning wastes of the Sahara. Unbelievable sight!

Two girls on a motorcycle combination. With their precious load of petrol and still more precious water, they are travelling steadily south, blazing a new trail to Nigeria. Thence through Equatorial Africa, taxing women and machine to the limits of endurance - To Nairobi and the all-red route to the Cape. Wonderful Panther!

Indomitable Blenkiron! Heroes of an achievement beside which every motorcycle record pales into insignificance: 14,000 miles reliability!"

Well, to be honest, the 14,000 miles did involve two different motorcycles! The mystery remains who exactly had contracted the aerial observation?

The Venture II on the return journey

Appendix B: Biographies
by Barry M Jones

Florence Blenkiron 25 October 1933

Florence's later years

Florence was quite an incredible, yet very private person and rarely talked of her African adventures even to her close friends. On her return to England in 1936, she put her love of motoring and adventure to good use by running private motor car tours, using her own Austin 18 hp saloon and toured all over the British Isles and the Continent. In the slack winter months she worked as a secretary and chauffeuse and in 1939, as companion/chauffeuse, toured the southeast and northern Territories of Australia, returning in November 1939 to enlist in the forces.

It came as no surprise that she found herself in a motor transport unit and in October 1940 left for familiar ground in North Africa with a unit of 56th Field Ambulances, ferrying wounded soldiers from the desert war to hospitals in Cairo. It is ironic that Jessie Hole also entered the ambulance service during the war, though as a civilian driver. Florence's mechanical expertise soon found her working as a Unit Fitter and in July 1941 was posted to the Palestine Girl Drivers' Unit where she took charge of 8cwt to 10ton trucks and armoured cars, travelling all over Egypt, Palestine and Syria. In September 1941 Florence was commissioned and her skills and leadership qualities were put to good use training others. She was Mentioned in Dispatches in 1945 under her rightful name of Margaret Blenkiron.

In August 1945 she moved to India to join the staff of the YMCA War Services Club in Calcutta, where she was placed in charge of transport. It was here that she met her future husband, a serving army officer, Kenneth Kingaby. They married in January 1946, moving to Bombay where she took charge of the YMCA War Service Club until it closed. When released from army service in June 1947, Kenneth became general manager for a large American pharmaceutical company and Florence organised large gangs of Indian labourers to renovate and reconstruct a derelict factory for use by her husband's company. They left India in 1955 and returned to England where they took up farming, but in January 1959 Kenneth suffered a coronary thrombosis putting payed to further strenuous farming activity and they moved to Thornhaugh, Peterborough to live on the farm for which Kenneth became Farm Accountant.

Sadly, in her final years, Florence had become an almost helpless invalid, confined to a wheelchair following a severe and crippling stroke. Florence Margaret Charlotte Blenkiron was a mere shadow of her former self when she died on 4th March 1991, at the age of 86. Her farm manager, David Powell submitted a detailed obituary to *The Daily Telegraph*, without which much of Florence's life would have remained unrecorded.

As a result of their parting in Cape Town, Theresa lost contact with Blenk. Florence's return trip to London and her subsequent life was to remain a mystery to Theresa. In 1986 she appealed in the British motorcycle press for contact with Florence in order that they could work togther on her *Rugged Road* manuscript. No contact was made and in the spring of 1991, I advised Theresa of Blenk's death. She then realised how much was now lost forever.

Theresa Wallach

Soon after returning to England in late autumn 1935, Theresa found herself virtually penniless having exhausted her funds on the return voyage and it is said that she walked the streets of London for some weeks, homeless.

Much to her dismay though, Theresa found herself excluded from the benefits of the promotions made by the expedition's sponsors. However, she had kept the detailed daily logs of the outward journey and had taken many still and cine films of the adventure (many of which were never developed!). I am sure that soon after Florence's safe return in April 1936, Theresa would have tried to make contact with her, but it appears no such contact was made for on 15th May 1936, Theresa presented a talk to the girls at her old school; Florence did not join her. The event was reported in *The Willesden Chronicle* and there was no hint of ill-feeling towards Florence; indeed Theresa was praised for her story, "told in manner simple and straightforward, with a strong vein of humour and no boasting.... she did not claim all the credit of success for herself and her companion." Curiously though the newspaper report does not mention Florence by name!

In her talk, Theresa remarked that had it not have been "for the kindness, hospitality and assistance we received from everyone we met on the journey, natives and Europeans alike, we could never have got through."

A fact which came out of this talk, but is not mentioned in her *Rugged Road* manuscript, was that one of the first people they met at the Y.W.C.A.

hostel in Nairobi, was a former classmate of hers, Evelyn Rix, who was on the staff of *The East African Standard*.

At the end of the talk she presented the school with the small silver Tuareg cross, formed by Tuareg craftsman out of a 5 franc piece, that had been presented her by Cpt. Favro of the French Foreign Legion at Agadez. In 1951, she gave an account of the expedition to the Sunbeam Motorcycle Club.

By late 1936 she was renting a small 400 year old cottage by the humpback bridge over the River Misbourne in Denham village, Middlesex. In 1937, with war in Europe imminent, she enlisted in a women's Auxiliary Corps at nearby Uxbridge, hoping it would give her the excitement and adventure she craved and so badly missed after the African crossing.

Her interest in motorcycling remained strong and dismayed by the lack of trade recognition that came from the African adventures, she determined to make more of a name for herself by once again aiming for the BMCRC's 'Gold Star' Awards at Brooklands. Although she approached motorcycle manufacturers for sponsorship, they each in turn repeated their earlier warnings that if she failed, it would only bring bad publicity for them. But fortunately on approaching Francis Beart, a prominent private motorcycle tuner of considerable repute, he agreed without hesitation when Theresa walked into his workshop and asked if she could borrow one of his tuned 350cc International Nortons for her to attempt the record the following weekend. "When Francis put a 'bike together", she later mused, "you didn't question it. You knew he was right!". However there was one condition. Beart agreed to lend her the motorcycle for £5 - a sum of money she hadn't got. Determined, she returned the next day with a borrowed 'fiver'!

Theresa wallach on the 350 Norton used to achieve the 100 mph lap at Brooklands

Even though Theresa had to stand on a block to mount the motorcycle, she soon learnt how to handle the Norton by placing her chin on a pad fitted to the tank and with her body weight over the rear wheel traction point. She had to ride high up on the banked turns and then drop down across the corners using gravity to increase her speed. On the morning of 1st April 1939, with rain falling, she took to the wet circuit and on her first lap reached only 97mph. On pulling into the pits, a puzzled Beart checked the machine over only to discover the ignition timing was slightly out. Satisfied at the adjustment, Theresa took to the course again and achieved 101.64 mph, gaining for her only the third and much coveted 'Gold Star Award' for lady riders. However, it is said that Johnny Lockett, who was Beart's top rider, was none too pleased at Theresa breaking the 100mph barrier for he himself had yet to achieve that target.

It is almost certainly from this event that Theresa later gained sponsorship from Norton Motors for her future American trek, however before any further adventures could be planned, war was declared.

War Service

Under tremendous pressure from the many Womens' Auxiliary units, the Government formed the Women's Auxiliary Corps in 1938 - it later became the Auxiliary Territorial Service (ATS). Not surprisingly, Theresa joined a Transport

Sergeant Wallach as a despatch rider

Corps and so began her seven years of active service. The lorry convoys which carried essential goods and equipment through the air raids and blackouts needed a special means of communication. As a keen motorcyclist she volunteered her services and was duly issued a War Department motorcycle, becoming she claimed, the first woman despatch and escort rider (or 'sheepdog' as she affectionately recalled) in the British Army.

In October 1939, she wrote a letter to *Motor Cycling* informing readers that she was "the only girl DR in the British Army". She went on to make a curious admission, "I can honestly say that I think more of my blue and white arm band than my Brookland's Gold Star" and went on to advise that she was in fact using two Nortons in her work, a 350cc ohv and a 500cc ohc and that she had taken up duties on an equal footing with other (male) DRs.

Her claim to be the first woman DR resulted in letters to *Motor Cycling* pointing out that several other women DRs were quietly carrying out their duties. Theresa responded, unconvincingly, by pointing out that what she meant was War Department DR's, wearing the official blue and white arm bands! This only served to dilute her initial claim!

From a mere Section Leader in October 1939 and after many hundreds of miles of convoy duties, her qualification as an engineer and her considerable motorcycling experience brought her rapid promotion to Sergeant Instructor and she now found herself training many more women despatch riders. She also helped organise off-duty motorcycle trials and events competing against regular Army riders - something forbidden to civilian trials riders due to petrol rationing! It was still common to present a cup to the best lady rider in such events and Theresa was to become one of the first women trick motorcycle riders in the Army!

It is said by others that she served for a short while in North Africa training agents of the Special Operations Executive in motorcycle skills, but she never mentioned this to me and indeed rarely talked of her war work.

It was not long before well trained ATS girls were routinely doing the work normally undertaken by the men who had been called up. By 1942, as a qualified engineer, Theresa easily passed the Army Mechanic Fitter's Test and became assistant to the foreman at one of the Ordnance Depot workshops where motorcycles and other equipment were prepared for despatch to the troops at home and abroad. The Colonel in charge, who was an electrician before the war, came up with an idea that Theresa should become a 'guinea pig' and report on the extent to which certain work could be taken over by women. She found herself working in each of the various departments, ranging from dismantling, assembly, inspection and dynamometer testing of engines. Few men ever received such a unique opportunity. The Colonel was so pleased with the result of his experiment that he happily reported that jobs such as hand lapping, would be better suited "to the more sensitive touch of a woman's hand"! Theresa soon found herself preparing reports to further the usefulness of women in the Army.

Towards the end of the war, the ATS Transport section was absorbed into the Royal Electrical and Mechanical Engineers (REME) and in 1944 she was transferred to one of their base workshops where she remained until demobilisation.

Test Driver

Her 'demob' finally came and with a return to 'civvy street', all she found on offer was a different coloured ration card and the prospect of seeking employment in a controlled labour market. It should be remembered that during the war all jobs were classified by their value to the war effort, some were essential 'reserved' occupations in which employees were exempt military service and such companies were scheduled under the Essential Works Orders. Those occupied on non-essential work were the first to be served with their call-up papers. To prevent the mass unemployment following wholesale demobilisation after the First War, demobilisation this time was a much slower and controlled process.

By chance she had made contact with W.O. Bentley at a British Motor Cycle Racing Club meeting at Brooklands in 1946. He allowed her to join his Research and Development team at Lagonda Motors in Staines. Bentley had lost control of his Bentley Motors to Rolls-Royce in 1931 and joined Lagondas as their Chief designer in 1933, soon after Rolls-Royce's unsuccessful bid for that company. His last design, a 2.6 ltr Lagonda model, had a new chassis, suspension, engine and solenoid operated gear selection. It was to be their first new car following their take over by the David Brown engineering company in 1947.

She found digs in a pretty summer cottage by the river, close to Staines bridge and a stroll through the boat yards soon led to Lagonda's workshops. When the great day came for the new car's test drive. The doors to the experimental shop opened and Bentley himself drove the new battleship grey Lagonda out into the yard - the only dash of colour was the red and cream trade number plate! It was to succumb to rigorous road testing by a team of test drivers, which included Theresa Wallach. Her first task was to build up some mileage, so she headed for the open roads towards Salisbury Plain, but the performance figures were quite low, so other drivers took their turn in trying to coax more out of the car. Tests were to be carried out on carburettor settings, fuel consumption and effects of overheating in town traffic, so Theresa dutifully headed for central London. Baffled though they were, the point duty Police officers never queried her constant driving around and around Piccadilly Circus!

She also found herself a pretty lane with a humped back bridge by a bend, between Basingstoke and Winchester, taking the car there many a time trying to go fast enough to get it to jump the bridge and test the suspension. Routine inspections revealed that the chassis had mysteriously cracked (she thought she had heard it go 'pop'!). She never did let on, but for her own safety abandoned further experiments at flying. However later on, another test driver had the front nearside suspension assembly come adrift from the chassis 'for no apparent reason!'.

It was not long after that Theresa, now fed up with post-war austerity, living off ration cards in a controlled labour market and in the depths of one the severest winters Britain had ever seen, her drawing room flooded and deciding the house wasn't big eough for both her and the River Thames, she decided to leave for adventures new in America. She had heard it was a motorcyclist's paradise with fast, wide roads and glorious weather. To the Americans, a motorcycle had evolved into a sports machine rather than a means of daily transport. She sold many of her possessions adding the proceeds to her post-War gratuity. Having secured her 'Gold Star' award on a Norton, she almost certainly sought sponsorship from Nortons, possibly with a business plan to promote Nortons in America and equipped herself with a new motorcycle.

The American adventure

In mid July 1947, she left for New York. Unable to book passage by sea for herself, she had already dispatched her 1947 Norton Model 30 'International', registration HOF 260, by trans Atlantic merchant ship; she followed 10 days later by aeroplane, landing at La Guardia airport, New York one day before her motorcycle docked at Brooklyn Harbour. Currency restrictions were severe and she was unable to take much money with her. Furthermore as a visitor to the United States she was not permitted to undertake paid work, but she had tentatively taken out immigration papers so that she could at least cover her expenses, so she was not too concerned with her immediate financial needs.

Her 500c Norton 'International' soon cleared customs. She had made no hotel reservations and her luggage contained only the bare essentials, lacking the usual encumbrances found essential by most tourists. Equipped with a sleeping bag and a pair of saddle bags full of tools, some snacks and riding clothing, she got bemused looks from customs officers at the lack of delicate skirts and dresses! A dock worker gave her a road map as he refuelled her Norton and soon she was on her way. With no interest in exploring New York City, she steered north along Route 10 through New England. The wide open roads and multitude of roadside shops, unrestricted by war time rations, were an eye opener and she was sorely tempted to stop every so often to feast on the splendid succulent foods on offer - what a contrast to Africa!

Each state in America had its own administration and bylaws. Whereas driving trough New York state was at a leisurely average speed of 50mph, she found in Pennsylvania that the minimum speed on their Turnpike Road was 70mph - a speed at which Theresa felt much more comfortable!

She headed along Route 15 to the Niagara Falls and compared them to the spectacle of the Victoria Falls in Zambia. She arrived at the falls in the early morning and spent the whole day there waiting for the floodlights to illuminate the falls in their full nighttime splendour. She later admitted that of the two, the Niagara falls were a bit disappointing. She then headed into Canada, crossing the St. Lawrence River over the Ambassador Bridge, riding alongside Lake Erie. The temperature here in late July was 96°F with a humidity of 80%. On 30th July 1947, she reached London - London, Ontario! She was entertained at the London Thames Valley Motorcycle club that evening, one of whose rules was compulsory attendance at their weekly meetings!

She eventually reentered the United States of America at Detroit, before heading to Chicago to meet some American pen-friends at their elite suburban home, on the north shore of Lake Michigan. The legendary American hospitality had taken its toll of Theresa's schedule and it had taken her 10 days to reach Chicago!

Soon after her arrival in Chicago, it became increasingly clear that Theresa's motorcycle and her habit of wearing slacks was neither welcome nor desirable in fashionable Chicago. Yet, she had no liking for their dainty frocks or attending social functions in keeping with their lifestyle; it brought back too many unhappy memories of her rebellion against the restrictive Victorian attitudes of her childhood. With an enticing map of the United States spread out before her, she decided to escape the oncoming severe Illinois winter and head off towards the sunny southwest.

With all her possessions packed onto the Norton, she was once more free to travel where she wished, camping when she felt tired or where the captivating scenery stole her heart. However, unable to bring much money with her, she was forced to do odd jobs en route and at Oklahoma, found herself repairing motorcycles.

Childhood tales of Hiawatha, Buffalo Bill and the Wild West lured her into finding out for herself if there really were Cowboys and Indians and whether, over the border in Mexico, there were matadors, picadors and bull fights too. She rode horse back with cowboys, camped near Indians and travelled in her own unpretentious way, wondering if travel could ever be like this again. On one occasion she persuaded the Sioux Chief, Black Horse, to pose on her Norton, but he would only agree if the mechanical horse was standing still! She also met Cheyenne Chief Big Snake and lived for a while with the Indians near to Buffalo Bill's final resting place.

Camping and trailing the wide open spaces, she sang ironic true-to-life songs such as *'Don't fence me in', 'Deep in the heart of Texas'* and *'When its Springtime in the Rockies'*! When she found herself broke in California, one winter, she signed on at a migrant camp and huddled together with dozens of Indians around a single radiator in a hotel outside a Hopi Indian reservation. She also earned money by giving talks on her adventures, mixing concrete, doing washing, fruit picking, farm work or working in garages. In two and a half years, she had worked in eighteen wildly different jobs, travelled 32,000 miles and enjoyed many adventures from New York to El Paso on the Mexico border, where much to her surprise she found a large dealership handling British motorcycles - she was in fact quite surprised to find so few British motorcycles in North America.

Theresa Wallach with Black Horse on her Norton

Theresa met many interesting people, native Indians, working Cowboys and saw much of America that today's tourists would never see. As with the African expedition, she tried to keep *Motorcycling* up to date with her American trek and how the intense freedom that she was enjoying in the States compared to those still suffering post war austerity, 'back home'. A brief article appeared in *The American Weekly* of 30th October 1949 which introduced the Americans to this remarkable woman. The opening paragraphs set the scene:

"The sun-browned woman on a motorcycle waved down the cowboy who was riding fast in the opposite direction. "I say there," she called out as he pulled up his horse short in a cloud of dust, "how far is the nearest town?"

He gazed at her in amazement. "Holy Mackerel, ma'am" he said, "are you alone out here on this desert?" She nodded, laughing, "but I'm quite all right. I've been all over the world alone - Africa, Europe, and most of your United States."

"Are you crazy or rich or what?" he wanted to know. "Maybe I'm crazy, but I'm not rich. I'm almost stone broke, but I'll pick up a bit of money some place. This is my transportation." She patted the handlebar of the motorcycle, "and I don't need much else".

"If people think I'm funny, I don't care. I love to travel and I haven't any money so this is the way I've decided to do it. There are so many marvellous places to see in this world", she laughed and nodded towards the dusty motorcycle, "we hope to get to all of them".

American Weekly

At the end of her American trek, her Norton was exhibited at the New York Motorcycle Show and it was here that she met Louise Sherbyn, an established stunt rider who was forming a Women's International Motorcycle Club; a contact group primarily for American lady riders who were touring Europe with their US Forces husbands. They mainly comprised members of the American 'Motor Maids' group, but following a second meeting at Daytona Beach, Florida at a motorcycle race in 1947, Theresa was invited to become Vice President of the WIMA, and in 1962 was made International Vice Captain of WIMA, a post she held until 1977. In later years Theresa became a member of 'The Retreads' - an international band of motorcyclists, a prerequisite being an age in excess of 40 years!

Soon after the New York Show, Theresa returned to London and rode her Norton 'International' to Norton Motors at Birmingham where they presented her with a brand new machine. She was truly able to answer questions about what life really was like in America, but before long the foggy, dank days and austere brick walls of London made her yearn for a return to the summer months in the States or the warmth of the African sun. It is not entirely clear when she did return to the states, she implies 1949.

Imported Motorcycles Inc

Back in America with her new Norton and her heart still in motorcycles, she tried to find employment within the trade without success and for a while camped rough in the woods which then existed behind the White House, in Washington. She still had several motorcycling friends in Chicago and moved to that city where she started repairing motorcycles. Doubtless inspired by the rarity of British motorcycles in the States, she thought of opening her own motorcycle shop but her bookkeeper told her that she couldn't sell motorcycles as she had no assets - he was soon sacked!

Theresa's determination to succeed won through and when the Indian Sales Company, which handled British motorcycle imports, got to hear of her, they said, "You are the kind of dealer we want. We can trust you and you know what you are doing with motorbikes". They financed and set up everything for her, to open her own dealership, at 2669, East 75th Street, Chicago. It opened on New Year's Day, 1951. She lived in a small flat above an all night cafe, in South Side Chicago, close to her grey walled motorcycle shop. It was to be her first permanent address since leaving home at the age of 17! In a *Cycle* magazine article of October 1956, Theresa writes that her present company "Imported Motorcycles Inc." was incorporated in January 1956, and it is not certain under what name she may have originally traded. As an incorporated business, she became President with Henry Steffes as Vice-President and his wife as the Treasurer/ Secretary. Her first Service Manager was Micheal Tipper who arrived from England in March 1956 but by 1970 she was working on her own with George Varney as her able assistant to help with motorcycle repairs.

Though probably remembered more as a BSA emporium, she also handled AJS, Velocette, Zenith, Ducati, Indian, Kawasaki motorcycles and Lambretta scooters. The shop was typical of so many 'family' run shops in Britain; a relatively tidy workplace showing years of history rather than a glittering showroom. She even had a piano at the back of the shop alongside which was a large glass display case showing her many trophies. The workshop itself was rarely busy, for she was very selective in her clientele, taking no interest in insincere riders or those with flashy 'choppers'. Her philosophy was that by turning away unwanted trade, she could concentrate on providing a better service to the dedicated motorcyclist.

Several motorcyclists recalled this unique Englishwoman and her motorcycle emporium. Many a time they would marvel at her dexterity in lacing up a spoked wheel, or of her stubbornness at refusing to refund a part which an enthusiast may have mis-ordered! Indeed she would willingly allow anyone to browse through her many factory parts catalogues on one proviso - they must wash their hands first - even if they were clean! What a character!

Part of the sales process involved showing the novice rider how to control and operate the machine. This was usually accomplished at most motorcycle dealers by the dealer riding pillion while giving instructions to the novice as they wobbled precariously down the street, then leaving them to their own fate once the money had changed hands! But, with her experience as a Sergeant Instructor during the war, Theresa was determined at the outset to ensure any new owner was properly trained to ride and handle a machine.

Theresa's concern for safe handling extended to motorcycle maintenance and many customers were impressed by the way their machines always handled better after she had serviced them than before. She never did let on for fear of ridicule, that her secret was to scrub off and polish the grimy leather saddle to restore smoothness to its surface, so that the rider unconsciously slid back along the saddle, improving handling and manoeuvrability at speed!

Her determination to provide proper training was also partly inspired by her own experience of the Illinois motorcycle license test, described later by her as 'ludicrous'! She almost failed the appallingly simple test by not using a hand signal to indicate a turn when none was necessary and also for refusing to answer a question on the State penalties for drunken driving! The disgusted look on her face was enough to make the examiner, who realised the stupidity of the test, to break out laughing as he signed the licence!

In 1962 her 'Motorcycle Riding School of Instruction' became an integral part of her motorcycle dealership. She used an empty corner of a parking lot in 75th Street Beach, close to her shop, taking care to ensure that on the first occasion a rider took off on their own, there was a fence nearby to prevent them doing too much damage to themselves! She not only taught the controls of a motorcycle but also the proper handling of one. Indeed she would not sell a motorcycle unless the new owner undertook a course of instruction from her! The course costs students $40 if they supplied their own machine or $50 if they used her BSA Bantam or for more advanced riders, her BSA 650cc 'Gold Star'. Tuition fees were reimbursed if they then bought a motorcycle from her!

With the demise of the British motorcycle industry in the late 1960s, Theresa concentrated more on her riding school project. She was determined to establish a new 'Standard of Higher Education' in motorcycle riding thereby fostering one of the greatest contributions to road safety. Her 'Riding School Project' was the foundation for her research. She wanted to give motorcycle riding tuition a leap forward by putting across a more academic level in keeping with today's high-tech age, providing better teaching and understanding of how a motorcycle functions in relation to the natural laws of physics; it was important that the novice rider understood the simple dynamics of posture, balance, braking and kinetic energy which could be embraced by the theory of the 'Triangle of Forces' - frictional resistance in tyres and grip, the effects of 'inertia' and 'kinetic energy', equilibrium and gyroscopic effects - factors which helped her to success in her pre-war racing and trials days.

She would pose the question, "Do you remember your first lesson in aerodynamics? You had to fold the paper carefully, getting the folds exactly right and the size of the wings properly balanced, otherwise it wouldn't fly?" The whole subject of dynamics in riding motorcycles was something that hitherto had never been discussed in motorcycle training.

The result of her research, was assembled as a training manual *Easy Motorcycle Riding*, published by Bantam in 1970. The BSA distributors in America sent copies of the book to all its dealers and Bantam Publishing produced a special 225,000 copy run for the Scholastic Book Services company who distributed the book to all High schools in America during the 1970s and 1980s. The manual aimed to encourage students to adopt responsible riding attitudes and to direct the natural aggression and misadventure in which teenagers found themselves, into a more rewarding adventure in motorcycle riding. *Road Rider* magazine said of the book ".. it would be worth buying just because of the attitude of rider responsibility.. (and).. contains plenty of information for learning the proper techniques of road riding.." The book was reprinted in 1978 and again in 1983 as a paperback, published by Sterling Publishing of New York and distributed by The Blandford Press in the UK. Theresa thought nothing of making a 2,000 mile journey by motorcycle to and from her publishers! In 1970, her local paper, *The Chicago Daily News* ran a very complimentary article on her, entitled "Uneasy Rider" - a most apt description. On occasions she appeared on "The Gary Moore Show", expounding her beliefs and theories on proper motorcycle riding tuition.

Easy Motorcycle Riding School

By the early 1970s Theresa had effectively wound down general motorcycle sales, concentrating on motorcycle training and only opened her shop to those who had booked for tuition. Selling a new motorcycle to a happy trainee was a bonus. In 1973, she closed her shop and moved to Phoenix, Arizona where she

Theresa Wallach demonstrates riding technique at her the Easy Motorcycle Riding School

dedicated herself to her new venture, 'Easy Motorcycle Riding Schools Inc.' and purchased and maintained training motorcycles and other equipment as well as arranging for a tarmac covered training area.

It is interesting to note the origin of the title 'Easy Motorcycling'. An influential Hollywood film, 'Easy Rider' had recently been released and it was felt by the publishers that the film's portrayal of motorcycling, American style, would be beneficial to the success of Theresa's work. On the contrary, Theresa was horrified with the irresponsible portrayal of motorcycling in the book - it went against the whole grain of her teaching philosophy, but she was overruled by the publisher. The success of the book spawned the Easy Motorcycle Riding Schools franchise.

Teaching motorcycle riding happened to be one of the most challenging and enjoyable things she had ever done. She had earlier vowed to study accident statistics and improve the general standard of riding. As a qualified engineer and expert trails rider, she set about devising a short course of instruction that would involve fundamental issues of dynamics. It was to be far more advanced than the usual method adopted by training schools which merely taught how to start the machine, drive it forward and stop, as if learning a language by hearsay, without ever knowing or understanding the grammar!

Even with her own extensive experience, nothing could compare with competition riding for picking up hints and tips from the experts and as a result she discovered the secrets which the professional riders could no longer hide! At Theresa's training establishment, each student would agree to be responsible for their own actions; if they didn't wish to accept this responsibility, then she argued, it was time for them to hang up their motorcycle helmet and walk away! The best skill she could offer was to help those who wanted to help themselves by developing as near faultless a way of safe motorcycle riding as possible. But determining what constituted a 'standard' of riding was to be her most formidable test.

She watched closely each time a novice mounted the motorcycle. There was a proper way to mount a horse and by observation she discovered there was also a proper way to mount a motorcycle. She learned much from and about her students; there was the 'dropout' who was an impulsive student, too anxious to get into top gear or who gave up too easily implying, "I don't want to learn, I want to ride." The dropout wanted the experience, but not the education. Then there was the 'reject' who had not only forgotten how to ride a bicycle but also the previous lesson! But at least Theresa found she could spot talent in most 'rejects' and with extra lessons and special tuition she soon transformed then into a 'graduate'. Graduates were the most adept and the most interesting to work with. After all, she mused, what greater and better reward is there than to be a proficient motorcyclist?

She studied the reasoning behind the skillful graduate and he (or she) in turn provided her with excellent feed back and a fresh insight into the project. It taught her many lessons. A jittery student exacted her patience like a baby sitter, while a 'smart Alec' demanded the tactics of a Regimental Sergeant Major!

Revision between each session was a time for self-reflection for both herself as instructor and the student. Every so often she held social events with coffee and doughnuts, where students, past and present, were able to exchange experiences and techniques with novices. She admitted that at times their collective minds were often better than her own! Their experiences ranged from urban commuting to long distance continental journeys, but they all agreed that their best lesson in motorcycling was the first occasion when they sat on and rode a motorcycle under proper tuition. They also told her that theoretical knowledge was the foundation for safer handling and together with her Riding School training, made them more appreciative of the lessons later learnt on the road. Her oft repeated motto "Check - Recheck - Recheck - Check" was forever etched into their minds.

One enthusiast from Texas, on returning home from attending a Riding School refresher course, telephoned her to say: "My bike - it doesn't feel like the same machine!" Of course the motorcycle hadn't changed at all, but his attitude to riding had! It helped that most of her students were of mature mind, often family men over the age of 30 years who still wanted a motorcycle, but had never got around to it!

Motorcycling for Business and Pleasure

Her book *Easy Motorcycle Riding*, proved to be a very good advertisement for her school and it prompted her to start another book. By 1986 at the age of 77 years, Theresa, standing a modest 5'2", her grey eyes still sparkling, should have been enjoying a well earned retirement! But she persevered with her Riding School project. She had however by now become increasingly disenchanted with the despondent attitudes towards motorcycling held by more and more teenagers as they sought their pleasures in motor cars. She realised that soon they and later generations, would miss the magic, allure and freedom that only a motorcycle could offer and she was determined to complete a new work on motorcycle training with the emphasis on self-instruction.

She was also determined to put pen to paper and write her *Rugged Road* manuscript recording her Trans-African adventure. With these literary works being of more pressing need, she closed her 'Easy Motorcycle Riding School' in 1989, but she kept her 125cc Kawasaki run-about and her BSA 'Gold Star'! Her new motorcycle manual, *Motorcycling for Business and Pleasure*, was written as a 'thank you' for the years of pleasure and adventures she had gained from motorcycling and training. It was intended to be a 'Self-Help Instruction Guide' to motorcycle riding, aimed at the novice rider who wanted to develop their skills in their own time, away from the established training school.

Her introduction in the new book began, "Many years ago, I discovered the thrill of learning to ride. Since then motorcycling has provided me with safe, economical transport together with independence and the pleasure of many touring and sporting adventures." She posed the question, "Why does a motorcycle, unlike any other machine, attract such attention and arouse such keen interest no matter where you are? Why are motorcyclists such enthusiasts? Is it the thrill of being astride the saddle? That glorious feeling of independence and total control over a beautiful piece of engineering; of rushing past the trees, swerving through curves, flying over the hills and riding with the wind?"

For those of us who are keen motorcyclists, I am sure we also often ask ourselves the same question, but how does one convey those feelings to someone who may never have ridden a motorcycle before?

Theresa was extremely keen to emphasise that 'Training' was not the same as 'Educating': 'Training' means following instructions such as "Do as I say - don't think for yourself", but when something new crops up, the novice is left in a confused dilemma. A dog, despite its considerable intelligence, is trained - it is not educated by its handler. On the other hand, 'Education' is the ability to think things out for oneself, allowing the student to use their own intelligence to interpret the situation - an attribute which training tends to subdue. Given knowledge and a standard riding procedure to work by, it was hoped these students would become more adept at tackling the exercises set in her book in a manner far better than she could ever have trained them.

At her Riding School, a beginner, given personal tuition and demonstrations of manoeuvres, could average ten miles and ten hours training over the course, but the object of her self-instruction manual was for them to learn to control the machine and perform the basic manoeuvres off road, no matter how long it took - after all, it is not the hours spent on the training but the work the student puts into those hours.

I read her manuscript with the hope of getting it published here in the UK hoping to foster a similar attitude to responsible motorcycle riding - however it would have meant much editing for the UK market. Having absorbed her work, I soon found myself analysing every manoeuvre I made on my own Moto Guzzi V-twin and can truthfully vouch that Theresa certainly knew a thing or two about safer and more enjoyable motorcycle riding!

Epilogue

Theresa was indeed a remarkable woman. She accepted that her independent lifestyle attracted few friends but in her own words, she needed to be independent and self-sufficient. Though she was an intensely private person and full of a sense of fun and good humour, she never considered herself to be lonely - to her that would be an admission of personal inadequacy. As she once said, "If you were not going to be like everyone else, you had to have the courage to go ahead alone - you can't go forward and take the world with you. If your environment holds you back, then you must leave it behind".

It is clear that she was at times quite a lonely lady. She had detached herself from her domineering father at quite an early age and rarely talked of her mother or brother, Charlie. Of Florence, she remained quite bitter until the time when she was told of her death and only then did she begin to open up. Possibly as a form of self-preservation, she remained adamant that she would never return to England, yet she loved to hear of life in England and spoken English - the BBC's World Service was a constant companion; at times my letters to her were akin to Alistair Cook's "Letters from America"! Curiously, though she loved her adopted home, she would never consider taking up American citizenship.

While tentatively editing her *Motorcycling for Business and Pleasure* manuscript for the UK, Theresa was emphatic that she was not at all interested in making money out of the project and all profits from the book should be directed into a fund, not a Trust, to promote 'education' in motorcycle training schemes. She was adamant that no-one should financially benefit from her ideas. The Royal Automobile Club and Auto-Cycle Union had previously run an excellent motorcycle training scheme and she would have liked them to adopt her work, but to protect her interests, she was determined they should retain her as a consultant; it never happened! Her caution was doubtless a result of the bitterness over the parting at Cape Town and the maltreatment she received from the press and those companies connected with the trans African adventure. In later years she closely guarded her privacy and intellectual property and was especially cautious of exploitation by the press, or others to the extent she rarely allowed private photographs to be taken of her ... just in case.

Theresa enjoyed a peaceful life to the end at Phoenix, living in small white washed bungalow below the Black Canyon Highway. It was her own, unique world of a 1930s Englishwoman, surrounded by her many motorcycling trophies, native American artefacts, a 400 year old Ivory framed manuscript of the Koran (doubtless from her father's collection) and her beloved BSA 'Gold Star' and the small Kawasaki runabout.

Theresa hoped that once she had got her new training manual and *The Rugged Road* published, she could then concentrate on her American trek memoirs, but sadly she never lived to see that day. After a short spell in hospital, she died peacefully at Phoenix on her 90th birthday, April 30th, 1998.

> *With the purr of my engine beneath me*
> *and the warmth of the high sun above,*
> *I'll go over the distant horizon*
> *along the country lanes that I love.*
>
> *Wild wood flowers and fruit will be growing,*
> *winding rivers flow down to the sea,*
> *On my revered travelling companion,*
> *I lay claim to a life of the free."*

Theresa Wallach

The first petrol pump South of the Sahara

Appendix C: The Rugged Road on Video

Theresa made a film of the trip using a 16mm cine camera. She used this film in edited form to provide a number of presentation on her return to the UK and probably also in the USA. This edited version still exists and is now held by the Arizona State University Foundation to whom the publishers are indebted for permission to have a copy made on video. The video is an exact copy of the film Theresa used in her presentation and has not been further edited. As can be seen the film and the book do not always seem to agree on the sequence of events! The following text is our best interpretation of the film with page references where the section of text can be clearly identified. It is a unique record of an amazing journey.

Mins Description

0.00 Map of the route – notice Africa is reversed left for right due to the film being spliced incorrectly.
View of Arab town streets probably Algiers

0.46 Scenes believed to have been taken at Theresa's home showing her father and mother, and the windmill.
The map is shown again this time the correct way round, and some scenes from the start, probably filmed at the Aldwych London.

1. 30 The escort from Algiers, the final petrol stop and the dirt road begins. The Venture climbs into the Atlas mountains showing an Algerian village below, probably Djelfa on the way to the highest part of the pass (*see p.21*)

3.06 An oasis town possibly Laghouat or Ghardaia or El Golea.

3.18 Camels and nomads investigate the The Venture

3.47 Leaving the oasis fort and heading into the desert.

4.15 Blenk watching a camel train and probably the Tuareg people.

4.42 Wreck of a car in the desert possibly where they stopped to repair the trailer hitch (*see p33*)

5.42 An oasis of some size in the Sahara. Exact location unknown but possibly Agadez

7.00 The Moslem festival celebrating the end of Ramada at Kano showing the 'reliable witness' galloping in. Sultan is presumably the man beneath the large umbrella (*see p 74*).

8.17 Now South of the Sahara in an African town possibly Kouseri because a river crossing comes next . However later in the film there is another river crossing clearly showing the local people helping to brake the outfit which is described in the book as happening at Kouseri on the Lagone River (*see p.79*) The film would indicate this happening after the equator crossing.

11.00 Dancer, possibly at the Seymour mission after the front wheel hub collapsed on the road (*see p 85*).

12.10 African village possibly filmed near the Seymour mission.

12.25 Blenk with the Pygmi chief Bondo in the Ituri forest (*see p92*), the welcoming dancing and children with elongated heads. Notice the boy trying to start the Panther with the machine in gear!

14.35 A view of the unfortunate chicken given to Theresa and Florence by Chief Bondo (*see p 95*)

15.18 Riding through long grass to a border which seems out of sequence as the Uganda border is described as having a five bar gate. Possibly this is the border to or from Chad.

End of Part 1.

15. 55 At the equator, doing handstands. The locals look a little confused! (*see p98*)

15.47 Riding through hilly country until they reach the first petrol stop since leaving Algiers at Lubero (*see p.101*)

18.25 Rutted roads and what appears to be attempts to mend the outfit after the accident. However according to the book this did not actually occur until they reached Taganyika. At this point (Lubero) according to the book, they have yet to arrive in Nairobi!

19.15 River crossing which would appear to be the one described as having taken place at Kouseri (see above)

20.20 Map showing route from Kampala South, followed by some shots of a man with elongated earlobes.

20.35 Signpost showing the road to Nairobi probably at Kampala

20.50 Bridge crossing a river probably after Kampala

21.15 The first major town shown on the film and probably Nairobi where they stayed at the YWCA (*see p107*),here they appear to completely unpack their sidecar under the watchful gaze of a monkey. This section is intercut with some shots of giraffe on the horizon.

22.00 Some more footage of the outfit broken down with a car nearby, almost certainly the breakdown described in the book. Notice the odd angle of the sidecar and front wheel here and in rest of the film.

23.00 This must surely be the tea plantation at Masaka (*see p 104*) which again is out of sequence according to the book as Masaka is well before they reached either Kampala or Nairobi.

24.08 The sign for the Great North Road and many hands make pushing easier in heavy sand.

25.55 The PWD maintenance signs in what was then called Tanganyika (now Tanzania). Again this should immediately precede the accident according to the book - indeed there is a shot of someone cooking rice as described in the book (*see p112*).

27.19 Tsetse fly signs and shaking out the bedding to rid themselves of any unwanted passengers! Again this appears to be out of sequence, Tsetse fly are referred to as being on the road towards Nairobi (*see p101*) not after.

28.20 Victoria falls, and unmistakeably so! This sequence also shows Mr Brew's steps (see p116)

30.05 Bulawayo and the monument to Cecil Rhodes.

30.17 Journey's end with the city dignitaries in Cape Town where Theresa and Florence demonstrate pitching their tent
Map of the trip and end of Theresa's film of their epic journey.

Interested in Panthers? Then why not join The Panther Owners Club? For further details send a stamped addressed envelope to:

Graham and Julie Dibbins
22 Oak St
Netherton
Dudley
W Midlands DY2 9JL
UK
Email dibbo@dibbotowers.demon.co.uk

Further information on WIMA (Women's International Motorcycle Association) from:

WIMA GB
Enterprise 5
Five Lane Ends
Bradford BD10 8EW
UK

WIMA also has branches in many other countries.

Lightning Source UK Ltd.
Milton Keynes UK
02 November 2009

145717UK00002B/2/A